TWELVE VOICES FOR TRUTH

*Confronting a Falling
World with Hope*

A Study of the Minor Prophets

Jack W. Hayford
with
Joseph Snider

THOMAS NELSON PUBLISHERS
Nashville • Atlanta • London • Vancouver

This, the third series of *Spirit-Filled Life*
Bible Study Guides, is dedicated to the
memory of

Dr. Roy H. Hicks, Jr.
(1944–1994)

one of God's "men for all seasons,"
faithful in the Word, mighty in the Spirit,
leading multitudes into the love of God
and the worship of His Son, Jesus Christ.

Unto Christ's glory and in Roy's memory,
we will continue to sing:

Praise the Name of Jesus,
Praise the Name of Jesus,
   He's my Rock, He's my Fortress,
   He's my Deliverer, in Him will I trust.
Praise the Name of Jesus.

Words by Roy Hicks, Jr., © 1976 Latter Rain Music. All rights administered by
The Sparrow Corporation. All rights reserved. Used by Permission.

**Twelve Voices for Truth: Confronting a Falling World with Hope
A Study of the Minor Prophets**
Copyright © 1995 by Jack W. Hayford

Published in Nashville, Tennessee, by Thomas Nelson, Inc.

Unless otherwise indicated, Scripture quotations are from the
New King James Version of the Bible, © 1979, 1980, 1982,
Thomas Nelson, Inc., Publishers

Printed in the United States of America
1 2 3 4 5 6 7 8 — 01 00 99 98 97 96 95

CONTENTS

· ·

Twelve Voices for Truth: Confronting a Fallen World with Hope (A Study of the Minor Prophets) is one of a series of study guides that focus exciting, discovery-geared coverage of Bible book and power themes—all prompting toward dynamic, Holy Spirit-filled living.

About the Executive Editor

JACK W. HAYFORD, noted pastor, teacher, writer, and composer, is the Executive Editor of the complete series, working with the publisher in the conceiving and developing of each of the books.

Dr. Hayford is Senior Pastor of The Church On The Way, the First Foursquare Church of Van Nuys, California. He and his wife, Anna, have four married children, all of whom are active in either pastoral ministry or vital church life. As General Editor of the *Spirit-Filled Life Bible,* Pastor Hayford led a four-year project, which has resulted in the availability of one of today's most practical and popular study Bibles. He is author of more than twenty books, including *A Passion for Fullness, The Beauty of Spiritual Language, Rebuilding the Real You,* and *Prayer Is Invading the Impossible.* His musical compositions number over four hundred songs, including the widely sung "Majesty."

About the Writer

JOSEPH SNIDER has worked in Christian ministry for more than twenty years. In addition to freelance writing and speaking, he worked three years with Young Life, served for seven years on the Christian Education faculty at Fort Wayne Bible College, and pastored churches in Indianapolis and Fort Wayne, Indiana. He currently enjoys part-time teaching at Franklin College in Franklin, Indiana. His writing includes material for Thomas Nelson Publishers, Moody Press, Union Gospel Press, and David C. Cook.

Married to Sally Snider, Joe has two grown children, Jenny and Ted. They live in Indianapolis, Indiana. Joe earned a B.A. in English from Cedarville College in Cedarville, Ohio, and a Th.M. in Christian Education from Dallas Theological Seminary.

Of this contributor, the General Editor has remarked: "Joe Snider's strength and stability as a gracious, godly man comes through in his writing. His perceptive and practical way of pointing the way to truth inspires students of God's Word."

THE GIFT
THAT KEEPS ON GIVING

One of the most precious gifts God has given us is His Word, the Bible. Wrapped in the glory and sacrifice of His Son and delivered by the power and ministry of His Spirit, it is a treasured gift—the gift that keeps on giving, because the Giver it reveals is inexhaustible in His love and grace.

Tragically, though, fewer and fewer people are opening this gift and seeking to understand what it's all about and how to use it. They often feel intimidated by it. It requires some assembly, and its instructions are hard to comprehend sometimes. How does the Bible fit together anyway? What does this ancient Book have to say to us who are looking toward the twenty-first century? Will taking the time and energy to understand its instructions and to fit it all together really help you and me?

Yes. Yes. Without a shred of doubt.

The *Spirit-Filled Life Bible Discovery Guide* series is designed to help you unwrap, assemble, and enjoy all God has for you in the pages of Scripture. It will focus your time and energy on the books of the Bible, the people and places they describe, and the themes and life applications that flow thick from its pages like honey oozing from a beehive.

So you can get the most out of God's Word, this series has a number of helpful features:

"WORD WEALTH" provides definitions of key terms.

"BEHIND THE SCENES" supplies information about cultural practices, doctrinal disputes, business trades, etc.

"AT A GLANCE" features helpful maps and charts.

"BIBLE EXTRA" will guide you to other resources that will enable you to glean more from the Bible's wealth.

"PROBING THE DEPTHS" will explain controversial issues raised by particular lessons and cite Bible passages and other sources to help you come to your own conclusions.

The "FAITH ALIVE" feature will help you see and apply the Bible to your day-to-day needs.

The only resources you need to complete and apply these study guides are a heart and mind open to the Holy Spirit, a prayerful attitude, and a pencil and a Bible. Of course, you may draw upon other sources, but these study guides are comprehensive enough to give you all you need to gain a good, basic understanding of the Bible book being covered and how you can apply its themes and counsel to your life.

A word of warning, though. By itself, Bible study will not transform your life. It will not give you power, peace, joy, comfort, hope, and a number of other gifts God longs for you to unwrap and enjoy. Through Bible study, you will grow in your understanding of the Lord, His kingdom and your place in it, but you must be sure to rely on the Holy Spirit to guide your study and your application of the Bible's truths. He, Jesus promised, was sent to teach us "all things" (John 14:26; cf. 1 Cor. 2:13). Bathe your study time in prayer, asking the Spirit of God to illuminate the text, enlighten your mind, humble your will, and comfort your heart. He will never let you down.

My prayer and goal for you is that as you unwrap and begin to explore God's Book for living His way, the Holy Spirit will fill every fiber of your being with the joy and power God longs to give all His children. So read on. Be diligent. Stay open and submissive to Him. You will not be disappointed. He promises you!

Lesson 1/The "Scoop" on the Minor Prophets

Journalists set out every day with their tape recorders, paper pads, and pencils in quest of stories. Whether the story is big or small it needs to be fresh, because old news, like an old fish, stinks. The challenge may be to find an angle from which an event has not been previously examined.

Before a fresh angle can be found, good journalists must be certain they are thoroughly acquainted with the basic facts of the story, which must not be distorted in the search for news value. The famous "Five W's" of a reporter (Who? What? Where? When? Why?) have to be answered before any other information can be sorted out and used. The "Five W's" establish the factual foundation on which sensational scoops are built.

Before you can discover a thrilling, life-changing spiritual scoop in the writings of the "Twelve Voices for Truth," you need to get the scoop on the basic facts about these prophets, their times, and their messages.

WHO WERE THE MINOR PROPHETS?

These twelve prophets who stood for the truth of God had little in common with one another. They did not act as a group. The few who were contemporaries gave no indication that they knew one another, although Micah does share one passage with the major prophet Isaiah (Mic. 4:3; Is. 2:4), and Jeremiah quoted Micah in a narrative section a century after Micah's lifetime (Jer. 26:18). Amos seems to have influenced Isaiah (Is. 5:11–13; Amos 6:1–7), and Jeremiah had a fondness for Hosea.[1] Even Haggai and Zechariah, contemporaries in Jerusalem among the returned exiles from Babylon who were committed to the rebuilding of the temple, did not refer to one another.

Some of the minor prophets give hints about who they were. Look up the following passages and summarize the biographical hints contained in them. (There are no hints for Obadiah or Malachi.)

Hosea 1:1–9; 3:1–3 *Obedient, Son of Basi. married Gomer, Had 2 sons & 1 daughter Gomer was an adultress*

Joel 1:1 *Son of Pethuel*

Amos 1:1; 7:14, 15 *He was a herdsman, a sycamore (fig) tree gatherer of fruit, He wasn't a prophet or a prophets son but God took him & told him to prophesy to Israel*

Jonah 1:1–12 (see 2 Kings 14:25); 2:1; 3:3, 4; 4:1–10 *Son of Amittai, disobedient to God's command, ran to Tarshish Jonah unconcerned of plight Jonah a Hebrew; believer of God who maid heaven prayed he obeyed, anger self pity, Poor Jonah*

Micah 1:1; (see Jeremiah 26:17–19) *Micah of Moresheth Living during Ahaz Hezekiah He feared the Lord*

Nahum 1:1 *The Elkoshite*

Habakkuk 1:1; 2:1; 3:16–19 *He was a prophet He was faithful to his duty His strength was the Lord*

Zephaniah 1:1 *He was the son Cushi*

Haggai 1:1 (see Ezra 5:1; 6:14) *as the prophet during King Darius - to rebuild temple*

Zechariah 1:1 (see Ezra 5:1; 6:14; Nehemiah 12:4, 16); 2:4 *Son of Berekiah, grandson of Iddo Prophesied to Judah*

WORD WEALTH

In some cases the names of the minor prophets have significance for their ministries. The translation or interpretation of Hebrew names is not always precise, but these are the approximate meanings of the names of the minor prophets.

Hosea	Salvation, Deliverance
Joel	Yahweh Is God
Amos	Burden Bearer
Obadiah	Servant of Yahweh
Jonah	Dove (see Gen. 8:8)
Micah	He Who Is Like Yahweh
Nahum	Comforter
Habakkuk	Embrace
Zephaniah	The Lord Has Hidden
Haggai	Festive
Zechariah	Yahweh Remembers
Malachi	My Messenger

WHAT DID THEY SAY?

The messages of these twelve who were for the Truth are as diverse as the prophets themselves. Some bore burdens about judgment and woe. Others proclaimed good news. Some spoke directly; others reported strange visions. Some spoke to Israel, some to Judah, and a few addressed non-Israelite nations. Look up the following representative passages and summarize the mood and content of each minor prophet.

Hosea 3:1; 6:4; 10:12; 14:4 *Forgiveness to unfaithful heart, Hope*

Joel 2:28–32 *Hope, Spirit poured forth before ened times*

Amos 1:2; 4:12; 5:4 *Vision of Israels distruction Seek God + they would spare them.*

Obadiah 15 *Justice*

Jonah 4:2, 11 *anger*

Micah 6:2, 8; 7:18 *awed by God's grace*

Nahum 1:3, 7, 8 *God is Holy & He will over shadow His people.*

Habakkuk 2:2, 4, 20, 3:2 *he stands in awe of God.*

Zephaniah 1:14–18; 3:14–17 *anger but then words of love, hope forgiveness*

Haggai 1:8 *God's plea for building the temple*

Zechariah 8:3; 14:9 *The return of Lord in Jerusalem*

Malachi 1:12, 13; 4:1, 2 *Destruction for most, love, protection for those who fear Him*

WHERE WERE THE MINOR PROPHETS?

You may have noticed in the biographical data that some of the minor prophets indicated their hometowns. Place of origin is one way to answer the "Where?" question. Place of ministry is another way to consider location, and the destination of prophetic messages is yet a third.

Look up the following references to places of origin for certain of the minor prophets and record their hometowns. Then consult the map, "The Prophets of Israel and Judah," to see these locations in relation to one another and to other biblical prophets.

Amos 1:1

Jonah (2 Kings 14:25)

Micah 1:1

Nahum 1:1

  AT A GLANCE

The following list arranges the minor prophets—the Twelve Voices for Truth—according to the destination of their prophecies.

THE SOUTHERN KINGDOM OF JUDAH	THE NORTHERN KINGDOM OF ISRAEL
Joel	Hosea
Micah	Amos
Habakkuk	
Zephaniah	**ASSYRIA**
Haggai	Jonah
Zechariah	Nahum
Malachi	
	EDOM
	Obadiah

Neither Nahum or Obadiah traveled to the foreign nations against which their prophecies were pronounced. They both resided in the southern kingdom of Judah.

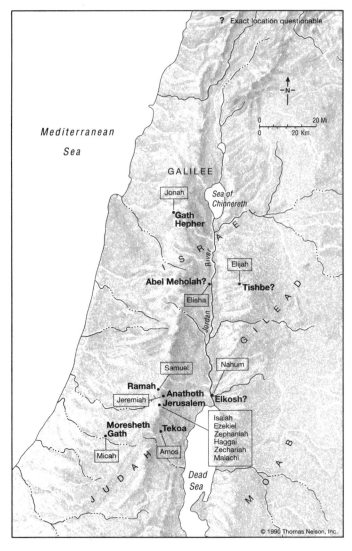

? Exact location questionable

Mediterranean
Sea

GALILEE

Jonah

Sea of
Chinnereth

Gath
Hepher

Elijah

Abel Meholah?

Tishbe?

Elisha

Samuel

Nahum

Ramah

Anathoth

Jeremiah

Jerusalem

Elkosh?

Moresheth
Gath

Tekoa

Isaiah
Ezekiel
Zephaniah
Haggai
Zechariah
Malachi

Micah

Amos

Dead
Sea

© 1990 Thomas Nelson, Inc.

The Prophets of Israel and Judah. From the Scriptures we learn where some of the prophets prophesied.

Samuel, who served as prophet and judge, used his hometown of Ramah as a base from which he made his yearly circuit to other places. Two other prophets of the early monarchy, Elijah and Elisha, had their homes in the northern kingdom.

Among the "writing prophets," only Hosea and Jonah were from the North. The exact location of Hosea's home and ministry are unknown. Jonah was from Gath Hepher, but his ministry extended beyond his homeland to the foreign city of Nineveh.

Some prophets had homes in the South, but prophesied to the North. Amos came from Tekoa but preached against the northern kingdom's worship at Bethel. Micah's message addressed Israel as well as Judah.

The ministry of several prophets centers on Judah and the capital city of Jerusalem. The messages of Isaiah, Jeremiah, Zephaniah, Ezekiel, Haggai, Zechariah, and Malachi span a long time period, but all concern either Jerusalem's approaching destruction, fall, or later rebuilding.

For some prophets, such as Joel, Obadiah, and Habakkuk, geographical information is lacking. The home of Nahum is indicated only by his designation as "the Elkoshite."[2]

WHEN WERE THE MINOR PROPHETS?

The "Twelve Voices for Truth" spanned nearly four centuries from the mid-ninth century B.C. to the mid-fifth century B.C. Look up the time references in the following prophets. Write down the names of the kings during whose reigns the prophets ministered, or the historical events that are named, and locate the prophets on the following chart, "The Kings and Prophets of Israel and Judah." Circle or highlight the names of the "Twelve Voices for Truth" on the chart so they will stand out more clearly for future reference.

Hosea 1:1

Amos 1:1

Obadiah 15

Jonah (see 2 Kings 14:25)

Micah 1:1

Nahum 3:8–10 (No Amon was an Egyptian city better known as Thebes, destroyed in 663 B.C.)

Zephaniah 1:1

Haggai 1:1, 15; 2:1, 10, 20

Zechariah 1:1, 7; 7:1

AT A GLANCE

THE KINGS AND PROPHETS OF ISRAEL AND JUDAH[3]					
The United Kingdom Saul 1050–1010 B.C. David 1010–970 B.C. Solomon 970–930 B.C.					
The Divided Kingdom					
Judah		B.C.	**Israel**		
Kings	Prophets		Kings		Prophets
		950			
Rehoboam 930–913			Jeroboam I	930–909	
		925			
Abijah 913–910			Nadab	909–908	
Asa 910–869			Baasha	908–886	
		900	Elah	886–885	
			Zimri	885	
			Tibni	885–880	
Jehoshaphat 872–848		875	Omri	885–874	
			Ahab	874–853	
			Ahaziah	853–852	
Jehoram 848–841		850	Joram	852–841	
Ahaziah 841			Jehu	841–814	
Athaliah 841–835	Joel				
Joash 835–796		825			
			Jehoahaz	814–798	
Amaziah 796–767		800	Jehoash	798–782	
Azariah 792–740			Jeroboam II	793–753	
		775			Amos
					Jonah
Jotham 750–735	Hosea	750	Zechariah	753	
	Isaiah		Shallum	752	
Ahaz 735–715	Micah		Menahem	752–742	
Hezekiah 715–686		725	Pekahiah	742–740	
			Pekah	752–732	
			Hoshea	732–722	
Manasseh 697–642		700			
Amon 642–640	Nahum	650			
Josiah 640–609	Zephaniah				
		625			
Jehoahaz 609	Habakkuk				
Jehoiakim 609–598	Jeremiah	600			
Jehoiachin 598–597	Daniel				
Zedekiah 597–586	Ezekiel				
	Obadiah	575			
	Haggai	525			
	Zechariah				
		500			
	Malachi	450			

WHY DID THEY PROPHESY?

The Lord motivated the minor prophets in a variety of ways. They were "Twelve Voices for Truth," but different situations called out very different applications of the Truth. Look up the following references and summarize the motivation of each of the prophets.

Hosea 3:1–3

Joel 1:2–4

Amos 3:1–8

Obadiah 10, 11

Jonah 3:1–3

Micah 1:8, 9

Nahum 1:2, 3; 2:8–13

Habakkuk 1:2; 2:1

Zephaniah 1:4–6

Haggai 1:2, 3

Zechariah 1:2–6

Malachi 4:4–6

Now that you have examined the who, what, where, when, and why of the "Twelve Voices for Truth," you are ready to look in more detail at the remarkable prophecies they wrote. You will soon agree that the only way in which these are "minor" prophets is in length.

1. David Allan Hubbard, *Hosea: An Introduction and Commentary* (Downers Grove: Inter-Varsity Press, 1989), 45, 46.
2. *Spirit-Filled Life Bible* (Nashville: Thomas Nelson Publishers, 1991), 1277.
3. Ibid., 488–489.

Lesson 2/The Truth About Spiritual Adultery
Hosea 1—3

The detective was given an assignment that ended with an extended stakeout of a suspect's home. Night after night nothing happened. One evening a pretty neighborhood girl joined him in his unmarked car. In a few days they were romantically involved.

He divorced his wife and married "the new cookie." Life was much more exciting with a younger, more attractive wife, and the detective looked forward to newfound bliss—until he was assigned another extended stakeout. Suddenly, his young bride, who had not been able to do enough to please her husband, flew into paranoid rages.

She was certain he was seeing someone else during the long hours he was away. The secrecy necessary to the case was proof in her eyes of his guilt. She began to follow him and made phone calls to check if he went where he said he was going.

The young wife knew how easily the detective had betrayed his first wife's trust, and she had no reason to expect him to be faithful to her. Adultery destroys the foundation for any confidence in the faithless partner, not only in the initial marriage but in any future ones.

The Old Testament prophets found adultery a particularly apt illustration of the nature and consequences of spiritual unfaithfulness to God. Old Testament Israel was often accused of spiritual adultery against the Lord. What happens between the Lord and a believer when the believer is unfaithful? What effect does unfaithfulness have on the believer's future with God?

SPIRITUAL ADULTERY DAMAGES FAMILY TIES

Faithlessness destroys trust. Once Gomer began to behave promiscuously, Hosea could not believe what she said or trust her actions when she was out of his sight. Similarly the words and deeds of the spiritually unfaithful lose their value before God and other believers.

BEHIND THE SCENES

If you compare the names of the kings of Israel and Judah listed in Hosea 1:1 with the chart of "The Kings and Prophets of Israel and Judah" in Lesson 1 of this study, you will observe that the period of time covered by those kings is more than a century. Hosea must have begun his ministry near the end of Jeroboam's reign and ended it early in Hezekiah's. Since Israel had not been conquered by Assyria (722 B.C.) by the end of Hosea's written prophecies, the time period reflected in this biblical book may be no more than twenty or twenty-five years.

What was the first prophetic activity the Lord required of Hosea, and what was the reason behind it? (Hos. 1:2)

Marry Gomer. Her adultry — Israel adultry

BEHIND THE SCENES

Did Hosea marry a prostitute, or did he marry a woman who became a prostitute? The phrase "a wife of harlotry" has been interpreted three ways: 1) as an allegory showing God's relationship with Israel; as indicating that 2) Gomer fell into an immoral life after Hosea married her; or that 3) Hosea knew Gomer was a prostitute when he married her. The simple direct reading of the text commends the third view as correct.[1] "Harlotry" is a plural noun. The faithlessness of Hosea's wife (and later her children) would be as relentless a pattern as that of Israel toward the Lord. Therefore, we must understand that the Lord's command to Hosea as revelation was that the wife he would choose was going to break his heart even as Israel had proven false to Him.

FAITH ALIVE

Guidelines for Growing in Godliness (Hos. 1:2, 3). Paul caught the essence of godliness when he wrote, "Therefore be imitators of God as dear children" (Eph. 5:1). Just as God called Hosea to live out His undying, eternal love for His people by instructing him to marry an unfaithful woman, He calls us to illustrate His Word and His very character in the way we live. A person's life is the most powerful sermon he or she can preach, and God calls us to act out His Word in our lives before the world.[2]

Hosea's wife Gomer bore him three children. What was unusual about the way in which their children were named, and what were the functions of the names? (Hos. 1:4, 6, 9)
Represent God's judgement on Israel. God named them.

What was the significance of the names of Hosea's children?

Jezreel (1:3–5; see 2 Kings 10:11, 29–31; 17:5–18) *God punished Israel because they forsook God's laws.*

Lo-Ruhamah (Hos. 1:6, 7) *God would no longer show my love to Israel. Judah would have mercy*

Lo-Ammi (1:8, 9) *You are not my people & I will not be your God.*

How did the northern kingdom of Israel commit spiritual adultery against the Lord? (2 Kings 17:9–18) *They worshiped others Gods. They deserted Gods law. They built high places. Burnt their children to Baal*

BIBLE EXTRA

The most graphic comparison of the spiritual faithlessness of the people of God to adultery and prostitution occurs in Ezekiel 16. In this chapter the prophet lashed out at Judah and Jerusalem for becoming worse in adulterous idolatry than Israel, who had already been captured and deported in fulfillment of Hosea's prophecy.

In his marriage and adultery imagery, how did Ezekiel describe the earliest encounters of the Lord with His people? (Ezek. 16:1–7)

How was Judah's relation to the Lord like a marriage—the best possible marriage? (Ezek. 16:8–14)

Compare Judah's faithlessness to prostitution.

Like prostitution (Ezek. 16:15–30)

Unlike prostitution (Ezek. 16:31–34)

How would Judah be judged for spiritual prostitution? (Ezek. 16:35–43)

How did Judah's spiritual prostitution compare with that of Israel? (Ezek. 16:4–59)

The judgment of the Lord on His spiritually adulterous people was never punitive. It was always ultimately corrective. A remnant would repent and from them revival would come.

After God's judgment on Israel, what kind of restoration would occur? (Hos. 1:10)

What was God's ultimate goal of restoring the northern kingdom of Israel? (Hos. 1:11; 2:1)

How did the hope offered to Judah (Ezek. 16:60–63) compare with the hope offered to Israel? (1:10—2:1)

BIBLE EXTRA

Peter devoted the first ten verses of 1 Peter 2 to various Old Testament texts as they applied to the spiritual status of the Christians to whom he was writing. Peter's readers were struggling with all sorts of persecution and troubles (1:6, 7) and needed to be assured that they were under the watchful care of a loving God who would not abandon them in their distress. How did Peter make use of Hosea's prophecy of restoration (Hos. 1:10; 2:1) to encourage his readers (1 Pet. 2:10)?

FAITH ALIVE

In what ways can Christians devote themselves to things in the following areas of life to the point of committing spiritual adultery?

Physical

Material

Social

Intellectual

Spiritual

Addiction

Others

What sort of chastening by the Lord is invited by the forms of spiritual adultery you listed above?

How does spiritual faithlessness remove a Christian from daily experience of the mercy of God?

How does spiritual faithlessness destroy a Christian's experience of relationships?

With the Father

Within one's family

With other believers

SPIRITUAL ADULTERY PROVOKES JUDGMENT

The Lord pronounced an oracle of judgment upon His faithless wife Israel. Later verses show that God's judgment was meant ultimately to be restorative, but while it was experienced it was painful indeed. Christians who give their allegiance to other masters also risk the anger and chastening of their Lord.

Hosea 2:2–5 refers literally to Hosea's attitude toward Gomer's unfaithfulness. Describe it.

Hosea 2:2–5 refers figuratively to the Lord's attitude toward Israel's unfaithfulness. Describe it.

How did the Lord propose breaking Israel of her infatuation with false gods? (2:6, 7)

What did Israel not know about the Lord in her life? (2:8)

How did the Lord find He had to teach Israel what she did not know? (2:9–13)

        WORD WEALTH

Baal (Hos. 2:8) literally means "lord" or "master." By extension Baal takes on the meanings: possessor, owner, obtainer, and (interestingly) husband. The Israelites sometimes became contaminated with the worship of a false deity of the Canaanites named Baal. *Ba'al* was also the regular word for "husband" or "master," and it was used throughout the Old Testament for human husbands or property-owning men (see Ex. 12:22, 28; 22:8; Deut. 22:22; Judg. 9:6, 7, 18; Prov. 31:11; Is. 1:3). Because of its use for Canaanite deities and because it implied ownership rather than relationship, God disassociated Himself from use of the term *ba'al*, asking rather to be called *'ishi*, "My Husband" (Hos. 2:16, 17).[3]

Why would the Lord remove prosperity and pleasure from faithless Israel in His efforts to reclaim her? (Hos. 2:9–11)

What was the danger for Israel of crediting her lover Baal with providing her with her prosperity? (2:12, 13)

FAITH ALIVE

What false "masters" are Christians tempted to trust and admire in ways that make them untrue to the Lord Jesus?

How might the Lord "hedge up your way with thorns" to keep you from pursuing false spiritual masters that would make you faithless to Him?

How might the Lord chasten you to convince you that you must never credit another spiritual master with blessing you?

SPIRITUAL ADULTERY HOPEFULLY ENDS IN RESTORATION

The judgment of the Lord on adulterous Israel was not a divorce. His desire always was that she would repent of her faithlessness and become a loyal wife. Hosea's marriage would complete the illustration of the Lord's marriage to Israel in this regard too (and also indicate the hope there is for any marriage, when both spouses turn wholeheartedly to Him).

How did the Lord intend to win Israel's renewed devotion away from her lovers and back to Him? (2:14, 15)

WORD WEALTH

Hope (Hos. 2:15) comes from a verb meaning "to wait for" or "to look hopefully" in a particular direction. Its original meaning was "to stretch like a rope." In Joshua 2:18 and 21 the noun form of this word is translated "line" or "cord." Rahab was instructed to tie a scarlet cord in her window as her hope for rescue. Yahweh Himself is the hope of the godly (Ps. 71:5). Here God's blessing on His land will transform the Valley of Achor ("trouble") into the "door of hope."[4]

How would the Lord know when Israel had become a faithful wife again? (Hos. 2:16, 17)

BEHIND THE SCENES

In Hosea 2:16, "My Master" interprets the Hebrew word *Baali*, implying "owner" or "possessor," while "My Husband" [Hebrew *'ishi*] expresses the affection of a family relationship. The names of the Baals were used in place names that tied the worship of the Baals with the land. Because it was materialistic, sensual, magical, and lacked ethical content, all traces of Baal worship had to be removed.[5]

What effects would the renewed marriage between the Lord and Israel have?

On the animals of the land (2:18)

On Israel's character (2:19, 20)

PROBING THE DEPTHS

Forgiveness Can Save and Transform a Marriage (Hos. 2:16, 17, 19, 20). Through the tragic story of Hosea and Gomer, God reveals *both* the depth and power 1) of His love for Israel, and 2) of the marriage bond. God describes His suffering pain and humiliation from Israel's unfaithfulness; and in obedience to God, Hosea suffers the same pain and humiliation from his wife's unfaithfulness. But God shows him how the marriage can be saved: through *suffering* and *forgiveness*.

This is one of the profoundest revelations about marriage found anywhere in Scripture. Successful marriages are not about perfect people living perfectly by their principles. Rather, marriage is a covenant in which imperfect people often hurt and humiliate one another, yet find the grace to extend forgiveness to one another, and so allow the redemptive power of God to transform their marriage.[6]

How would the renewed marriage vows between the Lord and Israel remove the judgments imposed in Hosea 1:4–9 and 2:6–11? (Hos. 2:21–23)

How did Hosea's continuing marital experience with Gomer illustrate the restoration of Israel to the Lord? (3:1, 2)

 BEHIND THE SCENES

Exodus 21:32 gives the price of a slave as thirty shekels. Hosea paid the price part in silver and part in goods. Fifteen shekels of silver was about four-tenths of an ounce. One and one-half homers was about five bushels.[7]

How were the restored wives to show their repentance for their previous faithlessness?

Gomer (Hos. 3:3)

Israel (3:4, 5)

AT A GLANCE

ISRAEL'S APOSTASY AND HOSEA'S MARRIAGE (3:1)[8]		
The stages of Israel's relationship with God are depicted in the prophecies of Jeremiah and Ezekiel, as well as in Hosea's relationship with Gomer.		
Stage	**Israel's Prophets**	**Hosea's Marriage**
Betrothal	Jeremiah 2:2	Hosea 1:2
Marriage	Ezekiel 16:8–14	Hosea 1:3
Adultery	Jeremiah 5:7; Ezekiel 16:15–34	Hosea 3:1
Estrangement	Jeremiah 3:8–10; Ezekiel 16:35–52	Hosea 3:3, 4
Restoration	Ezekiel 16:53–63	Hosea 3:5

FAITH ALIVE

How do you think the Lord draws back to Himself Christians who are flirting with other spiritual masters?

What place do you think formal recommitments (like that in Hosea 2:18–20) should play in the return of an unfaithful Christian to his Lord?

How can a Christian who has been unfaithful to the Lord express his or her gratitude for a restored relationship with God?

1. *Spirit-Filled Life Bible* (Nashville: Thomas Nelson Publishers, 1991), 1258, note on Hos. 1:2.

2. Ibid., 1273, "Truth-in-Action through Hosea."

3. Ibid., 1259, "Word Wealth: Hos. 2:8 baal."

4. Ibid., 1260, "Word Wealth: Hos. 2:15 hope."

5. Ibid., note on Hos. 2:16, 17.

6. Ibid., "Kingdom Dynamics: Forgiveness Can Save and Transform a Marriage, Hos. 2:16, 19, 20."

7. Ibid., 1261, note on Hos. 3:2.

8. Ibid., chart on "Israel's Apostasy and Hosea's marriage."

Lesson 3/The Truth About the Love of God
Hosea 4—14

The man loved his oldest daughter as much as his other children. He loved her when the police caught her shoplifting. He loved her when she claimed to worship the devil and collected occult paraphernalia. He loved her while her drug use worsened. He loved her when she seduced a married man in the neighborhood.

The man loved his oldest daughter as much as his other children when he cut off her allowance and took away her car keys. He loved her when he let her experience prison. He loved her when he committed her for institutional psychiatric care. He loved her when he finally made her move from his home and fend for herself.

For a long time the oldest daughter thought her father hated her. Years later after she was much used and abused, she realized who loved her, and she went home.

GOD CARES FOR COVENANT BREAKERS

Hosea could have coined the phrase "God hates the sin but loves the sinner." Hosea prophesied about a people who needed to hear of the love of God, of a God who wanted to tell them, and of the unique way God chose to demonstrate His love to His people. The people thought that love could be bought (8:9), that love was the pursuit of self-gratification (2:5), and that loving unworthy objects could bring positive benefits (9:10). Hosea 4—14 elaborates on the awful spiritual adultery of Israel and Judah, and the insistent love of God that seeks restoration. God wanted Israel to know His love, which reached out for unlikely and unworthy objects (11:1), which guided with gentle discipline (11:4), and which persisted in spite of the people's running and resisting (11:8).[1] Three times in these chapters, Hosea cycles through the progression of sin, judgment, and future salvation. The first cycle appears in Hosea 4:1—6:3.

What charge was God forced to bring against the people He loved? (Hos. 4:1, 2) *There is no truth, mercy & didn't love God.*

What would result from the great sin of Israel? (4:3) *Everything would die. (animals, fish, birds, plants)*

What was the contribution of the priests of Israel to the offense of the nation? (4:4–6) *They didn't know God or the laws.*

How did God promise to deal with the faithless priests of Israel? (4:7–10) *They would not prosper in anything they did.*

How had spiritual adultery enslaved the hearts of Israel? (4:11–13) *They turned to idols*

What other sinful practices flourished in Israel after spiritual adultery with idols had become commonplace? (4:14, 16–19) *They used prostitution, harlots etc.*

BEHIND THE SCENES

In Hosea 4:15 the prophet appealed to Judah not to imitate Israel in spiritual adultery and all of its associated evils. Gilgal and Beth Aven, centers of the idolatrous worship of the northern kingdom, were to be avoided if Judah was to escape Israel's fate. Beth Aven is a code name by the prophet for Bethel. Bethel means "the house of God" (see Gen. 28:17, 19), but Beth Aven means "the house of evil." Further, Judah was warned against associating the name of the Lord with any vow made in a corrupt Israelite worship center.

BEHIND THE SCENES

In Hosea 4:17 the prophet first referred to the nation of Israel by the name of Ephraim, the most prominent tribe of the northern ten tribes. Through the remainder of the book, Ephraim is Hosea's favorite title for Israel. If you locate the many place names mentioned in Hosea on the maps in the back of your Bible or in a Bible atlas, you will see that Ephraim was the focus of spiritual adultery in Israel.

What groups share the blame for the spiritual adultery of the northern kingdom? (Hos. 5:1) *The priests, & rulers & leaders.*

How did the spiritual adultery of Ephraim influence others to be faithless to the Lord? (5:3–5) *They caused the others to follow their example*

BIBLE EXTRA

The Spirit of Harlotry (Hos. 4:14; 5:4). The Book of Hosea teaches . . . [that] negative things happen when the Holy Spirit is missing from a life. Twice Hosea uses the phrase "the spirit of harlotry" (4:14; 5:4), and tells the consequences of being filled with an unholy spirit. Like Paul in Ephesians, Hosea connects such a spirit with wine, which enslaves the heart. This spirit of harlotry also causes people to stray into false ways and false worship in contrast to the Holy Spirit who guides us in true ways and true worship (4:11–13; Eph. 5:17–21). John records the words of Jesus concerning the ministry of the Holy Spirit who will witness to Christ; on the other hand, the spirit of harlotry keeps people from knowing God (5:4; John 15:26).[2]

What were the consequences of spiritual adultery for Israel in each of these areas? (Hos. 5:6, 7)

Sacrifice *So won't be found*

Children *disappear*

What were the political problems facing Israel and Judah because of spiritual adultery? (5:8–12) *These lowest of thieves*

What solution did Israel seek in response to its political danger? (5:13) *They turned to Assyria & There was no help.*

What would the judgment of the Lord on Israel for spiritual adultery be like? (5:14) *Like a lion tearing at them*

What response to judgment did the Lord desire from Israel? (5:15) *Acknolege their sins & seek Him*

FAITH ALIVE

Steps to Dealing with Sin (Hos. 5:15). Give sin no place to develop in your life. A fallow heart is excellent soil in which to cultivate sin. Deal with sin quickly and ruthlessly whenever it is found. Do not be lulled to sleep by those who claim God does not care about obedience. He looks for those who obey His Word and honor it by their behavior.

Recognize that God often allows misery into the lives of His people to cause them to seek Him earnestly. Be quick to admit your guilt of sin. Do not deny that you are a sinner. Confess, repent, and be restored to God.[3]

How is the Lord's desire expressed in Hosea 5:15 fulfilled in the prophetic response of Israel in 6:1–3? *They acknowledged & confessed their sins .*

How do the prophetic words of repentance contained in Hosea 6:1–3 indicate that Israel would one day understand the love of God expressed through His judgment?

The 3rd day He will raise them up & restore them

 ### FAITH ALIVE

How can willful covenant breakers in the church influence other Christians to be untrue to the Lord? *Hipocrits Bad examples*

What attitudes expressed in Hosea 6:1–3 seem most pertinent to Christians repenting of faithlessness?

His merciful, loving, forgiving

✳ GOD'S LOVE RELUCTANTLY PUNISHES COVENANT BREAKERS

The second cycle of sin, judgment, and future salvation occupies Hosea 6:4—11:11. This lengthy portion of Hosea's prophecy emphasizes the judgment awaiting Israel (and Judah) as spiritual adulterers. The prophet also enlarges on the intensity of the Lord's love for His rebellious "wife."

Describe the Lord's complaint against Israel and Judah in each of these areas. (Hos. 6:4–11)

Faithfulness

The covenant

The priests

Defilement

What was the heart of the prophetic message to Israel and Judah? (Hos. 6:6)

BEHIND THE SCENES

The priests (Hos. 6:9), intended to bring blessing and a way of life to those they served, have instead taken advantage of the people and led them into deadly paths. Shechem, designated a city of refuge (Josh. 20:7), became the scene of murder.[4]

What is revealed about the iniquity of Ephraim (Israel) in each of these sections of Hosea 7?

The robbery section (vv. 1–3)

The baking section (vv. 4–10)

The silly dove section (vv. 11, 12)

The "woe!" section (vv. 13–16)

BEHIND THE SCENES

Samaria (Hos. 7:1) was the capital city of the northern kingdom of Israel (see 1 Kin. 16:24). Situated in the hill country of Ephraim, Samaria had become a wealthy city (22:39; see Amos 3:15) and a center of Baal worship (1 Kin. 16:32). Except for the temple of Solomon, Jerusalem could not rival Samaria for wealth or importance.

What is revealed about the judgment awaiting Israel in these sections of Hosea 8?

The tool of judgment (vv. 1–3)

Covenant breaking (vv. 4–6)

Foreign alliances (vv. 7–10)

False worship (vv. 11–14)

WORD WEALTH

Trumpet (Hos. 8:1) translates *shofar*, which means a wind instrument made from a curved animal horn. The *shofar* is mentioned 72 times in the Old Testament, first in Exodus 19:16, 19, and 20:18 where a trumpet sounded at Mount Sinai, heralding the Lord's descent (19:20) and the giving of the Law. In the account of the fall of Jericho in Joshua 6:1–20, *shofar* appears 14 times. In Ezekiel 33:2–9, the sound of a trumpet (which warns a city of danger) is compared to the prophet's voice. The *shofar* was sounded not only as a call to arms but also to herald the Day of Atonement, the Year of Jubilee, and events such as the return of the ark (see Lev. 25:9; 2 Sam. 6:15).[5]

The Lord threatened Israel with exile in Assyria (Hos. 9:1–3), an exile comparable to their historic enslavement in Egypt (see 7:16; 8:13). What did the prophet predict would become of Israel's worship during exile? (Hos. 9:3–6)

BEHIND THE SCENES

Assyria was the empire that dominated the Middle East from the ninth through the seventh centuries B.C. Its capital was Nineveh and its home territory occupied the land between the Tigris and Euphrates Rivers in the northern part of modern Iraq.

The Assyrian empire eventually stretched from the Persian Gulf up through Mesopotamia and down through Palestine to include Egypt. Assyria was aggressive and brutal in its dealings with its subject peoples. It liked to swap populations among new conquests to disrupt social patterns and prevent rebellions (see 2 Kin. 17:6, 24). Israel fell to Assyria in 722 B.C. Judah was threatened by Assyria but saved by the Lord's intervention (2 Kin. 18:13, 17; 19:35–37).

How did Israel receive Hosea's warning of exile? (Hos. 9:7–9)

What did Hosea say about the impending judgment on Israel by means of the image of "grapes in the wilderness"? (Hos. 9:10–17)

Past

Present

Future

Express for today what Hosea would say to us about judgment for loving that which is unworthy of our love. (9:10)

What did Hosea say about the impending judgment on Israel by means of the image of a luxuriant "vine"? (Hos. 10:1–10)

Idolatry in general (vv. 1–4)

Beth Aven (Bethel) and Gibeah in particular (vv. 5–10)

BEHIND THE SCENES

Jeroboam had led a rebellion against Rehoboam, the son of Solomon, and established the northern kingdom of Israel in 931 B.C. as a rival to the Davidic dynasty ruling in Jerusalem over Judah. In order to break the spiritual unity of the Hebrew people, Jeroboam set up gold calves in Bethel and Dan, the southern and northern extremities of Israel, to mark them as centers of worship in place of the temple in Jerusalem (2 Kin. 12:26–33).

What did Hosea say about the impending judgment on Israel by means of the image of "a trained heifer"? (Hos. 10:11–15) *It is trained to plow*

What should have been (vv. 11a, 12)
They should have sowed righteousness & sought the Lord.
What actually had been (vv. 13–15)
They lived wicked lies, iniquity

What does Hosea say are the inherent dangers of trusting in our own way? (10:13) *Deceived by their strength & power*

What should we do instead? *Trust & Depend on God*

How can we depend on the presence of the Holy Spirit in our lives to see this accomplished? *The H. S. is always with us & He will direct & keep us IF we let Him & listen*

How had the Lord shown His parental love and how had Israel responded to it?

Historically (Hos. 11:1–4) *Taught them to walk, led with tender cords of love.*

At the time of Hosea (5–7) *They are going to be ruled by other countries, they will not be heard & saved.*

KINGDOM EXTRA

God's Nurturing Heart in Parents Flows to Children (Hos. 11:1, 3, 4). God reveals Himself as a Father who is tender, close to His children, and sensitive to their needs—teaching, encouraging, helping, and healing them. Growing up is not something that He leaves to chance. He is a God who conscientiously *nurtures* His children. God's heart toward His children is tenderly portrayed in the meaning behind Hosea's name. *Hoshea* means "Deliverer" or "Helper." The Hebrew root *yasha* indicates that deliverance or help is freely and openly offered, providing a haven of safety for every child of God.

This is the biblical model for parents: God entrusts children to parents, allowing His own nurturing heart to flow through them to the children.[6]

Describe God's attitude toward Ephraim in Hosea 11:1–9. *He loves them but He must punish their disobedience. An unfailing love He will be there even in their punishment.*

How did the love of God for Israel affect His judgment on them for their persistent spiritual adultery? (Hos. 11:8, 9) *He would not allow them to be destroyed. He loved them.*

What hope did Israel have because of the Lord's love? (Hos. 11:10, 11; see images in 5:14 and 7:11, 12) *He promised to bring them home after their punishment & repentence.*

FAITH ALIVE

What are some ways in which you believe you have experienced the chastening of God in your life because of sin or foolishness?

How did the love of God come to your life through these acts of chastening by God?

During the chastening *I see my errors. They become very obvious*

As a result of the chastening *I am able to restore my relationship with God.*

GOD'S LOVE RESCUES THE PUNISHED

The third cycle of sin, judgment, and future salvation reaches from Hosea 11:12 to the end of the book. The first cycle in Hosea 4:1—6:3 highlighted sin. The second cycle (6:4—11:11) highlighted judgment. The final cycle adds intensity to all of the elements but highlights future salvation.

What were the conditions of Israel and Judah at the time Hosea spoke his prophecies? (Hos. 11:12—12:2a)

Israel *lie to God*

Judah *Unruly.*

What had the Lord done for Jacob early in his life, and how had Israel departed from Jacob's ways?

Jacob (Hos. 12:2b–6) *Jacob always sought God.*

Israel (Ephraim in Hos. 12:7, 8)
He relies on himself, his riches not God.

What would be the results for Israel of forgetting the love of God shown through the lives of Jacob and the patriarchs? (Hos. 12:9–11) *They will live in tents. Their alters would be piles of stone.*

Contrast the blessing of God on Israel in the past with the danger facing them in the days of Hosea. (Hos. 12:12–14)

Past blessings *Brought Israel out of Egypt.*

Present dangers *Be taken over again by other countries.*

✱ ✱ Describe the fate awaiting Israel (Ephraim) because of her spiritual adultery according to each of these areas.

Ephraim's corruption (Hos. 13:1–3) *Human sacrifice to Baal*

God's newfound fierceness (Hos. 13:4–8) *Like wild beasts God will fall on them*

Ephraim's only hope (Hos. 13:9–11, 14) *God will ransom them from the grave.*

Ephraim's destruction (Hos. 13:12, 13, 15, 16) *God will have no compassion. ~~Drought~~ Drought.*

KINGDOM EXTRA

The King Breaks the Power of Death (Hos. 13:14). God will not only release people from the power of the grave and death (Hos. 13:14), but He will also take away the threat of death. God can bring back His people from certain extinction in a land of exile in Hosea's time; and, as Paul indicates in 1 Corinthians 15:15, God can once and for all remove the abiding menace of death on the basis of the victory won through the resurrection of Christ.[7]

Hosea 14 pictures the final and complete restoration of repentant Israel through the love of God. How does Hosea foresee the responses of the two parties to one another? (Hos. 14:1–3)

The Lord's call *Return to Him & ask forgiveness*

Israel's response *They repent & realize that only God is their salvation*

In Hosea 14:4–9, the Lord and Israel renew their vows to one another in the future kingdom of God. What does each promise the other?

The Lord *love them freely*

Israel *God's way right + if you don't follow there is TROUBLE!*

BEHIND THE SCENES

In Hosea 14:5–8 the prophet employs a series of examples from nature to show how God will restore His people with fruitfulness (the lily), stability (roots like the cedars of Lebanon), beauty (olive tree), and fragrance (wine). Then God Himself promises to be an evergreen place of shade (cypress tree).[8]

FAITH ALIVE

What kind of characteristics does a Christian need to respond positively to the loving chastening of the Lord?

Humble, teachable spirit etc.

What sorts of characteristics can cause a sinning Christian to reject the loving chastening of the Lord? *Stubboreness rebellion, pride*

How does the Lord deal with us when we resist His chastening and accuse Him of being against us? *Lets us go our own way. Testing & trials*

What should the Lord's forgiveness of spiritual adulterers teach us about forgiveness of those who betray our trust? *If God can forgive us & Israel & we should forgive others.*

1. *Spirit-Filled Life Bible* (Nashville: Thomas Nelson Publishers, 1991), 1256, "Introduction: Content."

2. Ibid., 1257, "Hosea: Introduction, The Holy Spirit at Work."

3. Ibid., 1273, "Truth-in-Action through Hosea."

4. Ibid., 1265, note on Hosea 6:9.

5. Ibid., 1266, "Word Wealth: Hos. 8:1 trumpet."

6. Ibid., 1269–1270, "Kingdom Dynamics: Hosea 11:1, 3, 4 God's Nurturing Heart in Parents Flows to Children."

7. Ibid., 1272, note on Hosea 13:14.

8. Ibid., note on Hosea 14:5–8.

Lesson 4 / The Truth About Judgment
Joel 1—3

Through his novels Chaim Potok has helped make intelligible to Gentile readers some of the rich variety within the American Jewish community. A generation ago a major element distinguishing segments of Judaism was the interpretation of the Nazi holocaust. Was it judgment from God? Was it proof God didn't exist? Was it just a calamity with no theological significance?

Needless to say, the survivors of the death camps could not accept the more casual attitudes of American Jews who had escaped the horrors. In *The Promise*, Potok described the arrival of the European survivors like this:

> In the years before the Second World War, the Williamsburg section of Brooklyn had been inhabited by only a few Hasidic sects. By the fifth year after the war, the neighborhood seemed almost dark with their presence. They had come from the sulfurous chaos of the concentration camps, remnants, one from a hamlet, two from a village, three from a town, dark, somber figures in long black coats and black hats and long beards, earlocks hanging alongside gaunt faces, eyes brooding, like balls of black flame turned inward upon private visions of the demonic. Here, in Williamsburg, they set about rebuilding their burned-out world."[1]

The awful suffering of the holocaust had to mean something. The Rabbi of Kotzk prayed, "Master of the Universe, send us our Messiah, for we have no more strength to suffer. Show me a sign, O God. Otherwise . . . otherwise . . . I rebel against Thee. If Thou dost not keep Thy Covenant, then neither will I keep that Promise, and it is all over, we are through being Thy chosen people, Thy peculiar treasure."[2]

People of honest faith try earnestly to comprehend whether cataclysms have theological significance. The prophet Joel began his message by interpreting a calamity that had destroyed the livelihoods of thousands of people.

THE LOCUSTS AND THE DAY OF THE LORD

When disaster struck the kingdom of Judah, the Lord moved the prophet Joel to look not only for the meaning of the disaster but to see in the disaster a foreshadowing of "the day of the LORD," which will dwarf all previous cataclysms. To whom did Joel appeal to respond to "the word of the LORD"? (Joel 1:1)

1:2 *Elders & all inhabitants of land*

1:5 *drunker & a drinkers of new wine*

1:11 *farmers & vinegrowers*

1:13 *priests who minister before the alter*

How did Joel describe the calamity that had come upon Judah?

Its uniqueness (Joel 1:2, 3)

Its identification (Joel 1:4)

 BEHIND THE SCENES

The locust is a jumping, flying insect, similar to a grasshopper. These four designations (chewing locust, swarming locust, crawling locust, and consuming locust) may be four stages of a locust's development, or a poetic form used to indicate the total devastation of the land. The best explanation, however, is that this is a description of four separate waves of locusts, each one eating what the other had left until the land is totally denuded of foliage.[3]

In what different ways did Joel view the destruction of Judah by the locusts?

1:5–7 *Like a lion with fangs, vines & trees striped bare.*

1:8–10 *virgin crying for the loss of her husband, loss of their fields*

1:11, 12 *harvest destroyed*

1:13, 14 *no offerings for God. – people must cry out to the Lord.*

In what ways could the awful devastation of the locust plague prepare Judah for the fierce wrath and judgment of "the day of the LORD"? (1:15–20) *They would have an inkling of the destruction, totally dependent on God*

BEHIND THE SCENES

Three events are usually associated with the day of the Lord: (1) The Old Testament prophets speak of judgment upon unbelieving Israel. "The cry on the day of the LORD will be bitter. . . . That day will be a day of wrath, a day of distress and anguish, a day of trouble and ruin, a day of darkness and gloom, a day of clouds and blackness" (Zeph. 1:14, 15). The fall of Israel and Judah to the Assyrians and Babylonians partly fulfilled such dire predictions of God's anger (Isa. 22; Joel 1, 2; Amos 5).

(2) Both Old Testament and New Testament point to Christ's Second Coming to judge the world at history's end as "the day of the LORD" (Zech. 14; 1 Thess. 5:12; see Matt. 24:43, 44). (3) At a climactic "day" still further in the future, the earth itself will be renovated by fire (2 Pet. 3:10–13).[4]

How did Joel describe the day of the Lord in Joel 2:1–11 according to each of these categories?

Natural calamities *fire burns the land, earthquake sun & moon grow dim*

Military calamities *swift & strong never stop*

Locust traits ascribed to an army *they keep comming straight ahead — nothing stops them.*

Human suffering *no one can endure it. pain or fear*

aug 7 →

BEHIND THE SCENES

The figure of the locust plague is merged with that of the coming "day of the LORD." Whether the impending invasion is from a literal army threatening Judah in Joel's day or from the apocalyptic armies mentioned in verse 20 or in 3:9–15 is not clear. Nevertheless, in remarkable poetic style, Joel describes both the terror of the locust swarms and the ominous presence of an invading army.[5]

FAITH ALIVE

What natural calamities in your lifetime have caused you to reflect on the power of God to rule and judge people? What did you conclude?

With what natural disaster do you think Joel would compare the day of the Lord if he were writing today? What points of comparison could he make between them?

GOD'S PEOPLE AND THE DAY OF THE LORD

After Joel established the awful character of the day of the Lord by likening it to a disastrous plague of locusts, he turned his prophetic attention to how the people of God should react to that dreadful Day. The fierce judgment of God does not hold the same terror for believers as unbelievers.

How did Joel instruct Judah (and by extension believers in the last days) to prepare themselves in anticipation of the day of the Lord? (Joel 2:12, 13, 15–17; see 1:13, 14)

   BEHIND THE SCENES

Rend your heart and not your garments (Joel 2:13). The tearing of one's garment was a common practice in times of grief or contrition. It symbolized a broken and torn spirit. Here Joel is calling for Judah to actually experience what the symbolism portrays: hearts that are torn with grief and the confession of their sins.[6]

Why is this a good approach for believers to make to the Lord? (Joel 2:13, 14)

What was to be the appeal of the repentant inhabitants of Judah to the Lord? (Joel 2:15–17)

   KINGDOM EXTRA

Steps to Dealing with Corporate Sin (Joel 2:12–17). Joel's prophecies explain how a people must deal with corporate sin. His prophetic warnings and exhortations are addressed primarily to the spiritual leaders. He calls them first to lead in wholehearted repentance and then to confront the people's sin. Corporate fasts and solemn assemblies to cry out to the Lord are some of the practices Joel recommends to deal with corporate sin.

Repent quickly with mourning when sin is discovered in you. Confess your sin and let God work in your heart. Continually turn to God and set your affections on His will and His ways. Call for revival. Enjoin the elders to lead in fasting and prayer.[7]

How would the appeal of repentant Judah be answered by the Lord? (Joel 2:18–20)

In terms of the locust plague

In terms of the future day of the Lord

How can the repentant and forgiven people of God anticipate recovery from devastation? (Joel 2:21–27)

After the locust plague

After the day of the Lord

     BEHIND THE SCENES

In Joel 2:23 "former rain" refers to the autumn rain, which came at planting time. "Latter rain" is the spring rain that occurs just before harvest. This outpouring of refreshing rain which renews the fertility of the parched ground prefigures the outpouring of the Spirit, which will bring spiritual renewal (vv. 28–32).[8]

With what supernatural resource will the repentant and forgiven people of God face the day of the Lord? (Joel 2:28–32)

What seems to you to be the significance of the distribu-
tion of the Spirit on men and women, young and old, free
people and slaves? (Joel 2:28, 29)

What do you think is the significance of the fact that
prophecy, dreams, and visions accompany the pouring out of
the Spirit before the day of the Lord? (Joel 2:28)

BEHIND THE SCENES

"All flesh" refers to every class of person, not every individual. As the repentance in verse 16 reached to the youngest
and the oldest, so this outpouring of the Spirit also reaches to
every age and status, to both men and women.

"Prophesy" means to bring God's viewpoint to earthly
matters. A prophet is one who sees and speaks for God.
Dreams and visions were the common ways in which prophecy
came in Old Testament times. The point here is that prophetic
ministry would be no longer relegated to a few, but would be
the characteristic of even the young men.

"Manservants . . . maidservants" are the slaves. This
was absolutely unprecedented. In the Old Testament there is
not even one instance of a slave functioning as a prophet.

In Acts 2, Peter sees the outpouring of the Spirit at Pentecost and the fulfillment of this prophecy. That this coming of
the Spirit was not relegated to the apostles and their contemporaries is made clear by Peter's statements in Acts 2:39,
"The promise is to you and to your children, and to all who are
afar off, as many as the Lord our God will call."[9]

WORD WEALTH

Dreams, *chalom* (kah-*lohm*); Strong's #2472; A dream; a vision in the night. The root of this noun is the verb *chalam*, "to dream." Dreams of various types are mentioned in Scripture, ranging from the product of one's imagination to the vehicle of God's communication with a person (compare Eccl. 5:3 and Gen. 20:6; see also "false dreams," Jer. 23:32). Many biblical figures, such as Jacob, Laban, Pharaoh, Solomon, Nebuchadnezzar, are known for having dreams (see 1 Kings 3:5; Dan. 2:1). Joseph and Daniel are the biblical champions of dream-revelation; each not only received his own dreams but also interpreted the dreams of others as well.[10]

 FAITH ALIVE

Dreams and visions are not just an Old Testament occurrence, but take place in the New Testament both before and after Pentecost. Matthew records God's speaking through dreams to Joseph (Matt. 1:20; 2:13, 19, 22), the wise men (Matt. 2:12), and Pilate's wife (Matt. 27:19). We see similar experiences through dreams and visions recorded of Peter and Cornelius in Acts 10 and Paul in Acts 16:9.

Has God ever spoken to you through a dream or vision? What were the circumstances? How did it affect your life then and later?

 KINGDOM EXTRA

The Holy Spirit: The Agent of Restoration (Joel 2:28, 29). God's work of restoration is a work of the Holy Spirit through the lives of those who have believed in Jesus and have been born from above (John 3:3). The prophet Joel foretold a day when God would pour out His Spirit "on all flesh" (Joel 2:28, 29). Thus, His power would be shared with all His people and not limited to one chosen individual. This explains why Christ told His disciples it was to their advantage for Him to leave them and go to the Father (John 16:7), because then the Spirit could be sent to indwell each of them, to fill them and to enable the supernatural works of God to be done through them.

Titus 3:5, 6 reveals that even salvation—the regeneration of the dead spirit of man and the cleansing that makes the new man acceptable to God—is the work of the Holy Spirit.

Finally, in Acts 1:8 Jesus tells the disciples to do nothing until the Holy Spirit has come. Then, He promises, they will be empowered to witness of Him and their witness will spread the Good News throughout the world.[11]

What will be the signs before the day of the Lord? (Joel 2:30, 31)

How will unbelievers be able to escape the terrors of the day of the Lord? (Joel 2:32)

![question icon] PROBING THE DEPTHS

The Holy Spirit at Work (Joel 2:28–32). The prophet sees a time in the future, "afterward," when the Spirit of God will be poured out "on all flesh." Young and old alike, both men and women, will experience this outpouring. The section of Scripture hangs suspended for nearly eight hundred years. Though the Spirit had come upon the prophets and priests, never had there been such a general outpouring of the Spirit. Then, on the Day of Pentecost, the Spirit came with such power and force that it captured the attention of the masses gathered in Jerusalem for the festival. Peter takes hold of this prophetic section and declares, "But this is what was spoken of by the prophet Joel" (Acts 2:16). A new age is born, the church is empowered, and now "whoever calls on the name of the LORD shall be saved."[12]

No event in Joel's time answers this prophetic section (vv. 28–32). It has its initial fulfillment on the Day of Pentecost when the outpouring of the Spirit began "the last days." Joel's prophecy will culminate with the coming again of the Messiah, Jesus Christ, and the subsequent end of this world. We are now living in these prolonged last days. The rising crescendo of violence and war that characterizes contemporary history should be understood as the beckoning of God for men to call upon Him and be saved.[13]

FAITH ALIVE

How have you found repentance to be a prerequisite in your Christian experience for the enjoyment of the Holy Spirit in your life?

How do you expect the Holy Spirit to sustain you in times of distress and calamity?

THE NATIONS AND THE DAY OF THE LORD

The terrors of the day of the Lord are most awful for the unbelieving nations who have oppressed the people of God, even if those nations were instruments of God's chastening at the time. Joel continued to use images from agriculture and refer to signs in the heavens.

Why must God judge the nations on the day of the Lord? (Joel 3:1–3)

BEHIND THE SCENES

In Jewish tradition "the Valley of Jehoshaphat" (Joel 3:2) is thought to be part of the Kidron Valley between the temple and the Mount of Olives. "Jehoshaphat" means "Yahweh is Judge." This, therefore, may be a symbolic place of judgment and decision rather than an actual place in Joel's mind.[14]

What was the Lord's specific complaint against Tyre, Sidon, and Philistia? (Joel 3:4–8)

What is God's proclamation to the nations for the day of the Lord? (Joel 3:9–11)

BEHIND THE SCENES

"Beat your plowshares into swords and your pruning hooks into spears" (Joel 3:10) is an inversion of Isaiah 2:4. There the weapons of war are to be made into instruments of peace. Here the implements of peaceful agriculture are to be made into weapons of war. The language is symbolic.[15]

What will be the outcome of the day of the Lord?

For the nations (Joel 3:12–16)

For the people of God (Joel 3:16, 17)

When the day of the Lord ends, what will be the outcome?

For the people of God (Joel 3:18)

For the oppressors of God's people (Joel 3:19–21)

BEHIND THE SCENES

The opening line of Joel 3:21 is difficult to translate. Biblical languages employed no punctuation marks (or even spaces between words), so it is sometimes difficult to group words into sentences or determine the kind of sentence. For verse 21, "another option is to translate, 'And shall I leave their bloodshed [the Judean blood shed by the nations] go unpunished? I will not.'"[16] Yet some interpret this line as announcing the pardoning of the nations who have now been judged by God and therefore can be pardoned. Others see this statement as indicating that all guilt can now be forgiven since "the Lord dwells in Zion." God's dwelling in Zion means that He has established His kingdom and all the enemies of His people have been eliminated. Thus the world to come has begun.[17]

FAITH ALIVE

From Joel's prophecy, what have you learned about the Lord's motivations for judging the unbelieving nations?

His own people?

How should the reality of the future day of the Lord affect your missionary zeal?

Your personal commitment to the Lord?

1. Chaim Potok, *The Promise* (New York: Alfred A. Knopf, Inc., 1969), 3.
2. Quoted in *The Promise*, frontispiece.
3. *Spirit-Filled Life Bible* (Nashville: Thomas Nelson Publishers, 1991), 1276, note on Joel 1:4.
4. "Day of the Lord." *The Revell Bible Dictionary* (Old Tappan: Fleming H. Revell Company, 1990), 282.
5. *Spirit-Filled Life Bible*, 1278, note on Joel 2:1–11.
6. Ibid., 1279, note on Joel 2:13.
7. Ibid., 1284, "Truth-in-Action through Joel."
8. Ibid., 1280, note on Joel 2:23.
9. Ibid., 1281, note on Joel 2:28, 29.
10. Ibid., "Word Wealth: Joel 2:28 dreams."
11. Ibid., 2016, "The Holy Spirit: The Agent of Restoration."
12. Ibid., 1276, "Joel: Introduction, The Holy Spirit at Work."
13. Ibid., 1282, note on Joel 2:32.
14. Ibid., note on Joel 3:2.
15. Ibid., 1283, note on Joel 3:10.
16. Robert B. Chisholm, Jr. "Joel," *The Bible Knowledge Commentary: Old Testament* (Wheaton: Victor Books, 1985), 1423.
17. *Spirit-Filled Life Bible*, 1283, note on Joel 3:21.

Lesson 5/The Truth About Injustice
Amos 1—9

American writer Robert Penn Warren contributed significantly to the southern school of twentieth century novelists. Penn Warren's most famous novel, *All the King's Men*, traced the rise of Willie Stark to the governorship of a southern state, his corruption by power, and his subsequent self-destruction.

Loosely modeled after Huey Long of Louisiana, Willie Stark began his political career as a county politician frustrated in his efforts to save the tax dollars of poor rural folk from the "fat cats" above him who counted on bribes as part of the political process. One day in Willie's town a school fire escape collapsed because of shoddy materials, and some children died. Townsfolk said it was judgment for not voting for Willie. Soon he represented workmen injured in the collapse of a bridge being built by the state and won compensation for them. Finally he successfully sued an oil company on behalf of small landholders who felt their mineral rights had been stolen.

When Willie Stark ran for governor, the "hicks and hayseeds" anointed him as their champion. Willie Stark became governor because he unrelentingly exposed injustice and embodied justice. But in the end, Willie Stark failed because he was a man without a moral compass.

The prophet Amos railed against injustice as fiercely as the fictional Willie Stark, but Amos was incorruptible. Amos spoke for God, and his attacks on injustice were rooted in the absolute justice of the law of God.

INJUSTICE IS FUNDAMENTALLY CRUEL

It's surprising that the opening charges against injustice all around Israel as well as inside Israel did not attack greed, abuse of power, irresponsibility, wealth, or any other typical trapping of injustice. Amos focused first on the cruelty of injustice. He saw in the behavior of the near eastern nations of his day the same treatment of other people that Cain showed his brother Abel in Genesis 4. Injustice is cruel.

How did Amos describe the nature and effect of the Lord's message against injustice? (Amos 1:2)

    BEHIND THE SCENES

Amos arranged his judgments upon the nations in a geographical-psychological pattern. Beginning with the nations on the four corners (Damascus to the northeast, Gaza to the southwest, Tyre to the northwest, and Edom to the southeast), Amos crossed the land of Israel twice and drew the circle tighter with Ammon, Moab, and Judah before pouncing on Israel.

The prophet began each oracle of judgment with a literary method known as graduated numbers or numerical parallelism: "For three transgressions . . . and for four" (see, for example, 1:3, 6, 9). This numerical system suggests the meaning "For enough transgressions . . . for more than enough." Similar uses of graduated numerals are found in Proverbs 6:16; 30:15, 18, 21, 29; Micah 5:5.[1]

What cruelty did the Lord accuse each of the following nations of as the basis for His judgment?

Damascus (Amos 1:3, Gilead was Israel east of the Jordan)

Gaza (Amos 1:6, "captivity" means commercial dealing in Hebrew slaves)

Tyre (Amos 1:9)

Edom (Amos 1:11, Edom was founded by Esau the brother of Jacob)

Ammon (Amos 1:13)

Moab (Amos 2:1)

Israel (Amos 2:6–8)

The Lord did not roar against Judah because of cruelty. What was the Lord's charge against Judah, and what do you think is its relationship to injustice and cruelty? (Amos 2:4)

Why do you think the roar of the Lord's voice originated in Jerusalem in Judah but withered Mount Carmel miles to the north in Israel? (Amos 1:2)

What sentence of judgment did the Lord roar out like a lion against each of the following nations for their cruel injustices?

Damascus (Amos 1:4, 5, Ben-Hadad was a Syrian king of the dynasty of Hazael)

Gaza (Amos 1:7, 8, the five Philistine cities were Gaza, Ashdod, Ashkelon, Ekron, and Gath)

Tyre (Amos 1:10)

Edom (Amos 1:12, Teman and Bozrah were the principal cities of Edom)

Ammon (Amos 1:14, 15, Rabbah was the capital)

Moab (Amos 2:2, 3)

Judah (Amos 2:5)

Israel (Amos 2:13–16 and the rest of the book)

What historical factors made Israel's cruel injustice more serious than that of the pagan nations? (Amos 2:9–12)

KINGDOM EXTRA

Guidelines for Growing in Godliness (Amos 2:11, 12). The rebellious and disobedient among God's people tend to actively discourage godly and righteous behavior on the part of others. God says He will bring severe judgment against these. God wants us to do all we can to encourage His people to seek Him and obey His Word.

Do not discourage godliness, nor put roadblocks in the way of those who pursue godliness and truth. Allow the full expression of the prophetic ministry so that God's people can be warned. Encourage the straightforward preaching of God's Word.[2]

FAITH ALIVE

How have you observed cruelty in the personalities of individuals who despise the law of God?

How have you observed cruelty in the activities of organizations, companies, and nations that ignore the law of God?

INJUSTICE ANGERS GOD

The prophecy of Amos is characterized by the formulae "Thus says the LORD" and "Hear the word." And when the Lord is ready to reveal His personal reaction to injustice—especially the injustice found among His own people—He is furious. "A lion has roared!" Amos said. "Who will not fear?" (3:8).

Look at Amos 3:1; 4:1; 5:1, 16 for the major divisions of chapters 3—7. How would you characterize the mood or tone of each of these four sections?

3:1, 2

4:1, 2

5:1–3

5:16, 18; 6:1, 3

 BEHIND THE SCENES

God has a special relationship with Israel, which is expressed in the Hebrew word for "to know." While God knows about all the nations, as Amos demonstrates forcefully in 1:3—2:3, He knows Israel in a special, intimate way, and shows concern, pity, sympathy, and care for her. Because of this relationship, Israel has a correspondingly special responsibility.[3]

The series of rhetorical questions in Amos 3:3–6 assumes that when certain results are seen, the observer knows what caused those results. The first five questions assume a negative answer and the last two assume a positive one. What hints about Israel's future are given by the questions?

Why was prophecy so prominent during the time of impending judgment of Israel (and later Judah)? (Amos 3:7, 8)

What is revealed about the anger of the Lord against injustice by His chosen people in each of these passages?

3:9, 10

3:11

3:12–15

What is revealed in Amos 4:1–5 about the anger of the Lord against injustice by wealthy people against the poor?

  BEHIND THE SCENES

The wives of the principal men of Samaria are likened to the cows raised in the verdant pastures of Bashan. Their desire for more wealth and luxury spurs their husbands to do more wicked deeds; thus they share the guilt of their husbands for exploiting the poor ruthlessly.[4]

What progression of chastening had the Lord brought upon unresponsive, wealthy Israel prior to the prophecy of Amos?

4:6

4:7, 8

4:9

4:10

4:11

    BIBLE EXTRA

Amos reported that Israel had experienced famine, drought, blight and mildew, plague, and military defeat as punishment from God. This was not a list of arbitrary calamities that Amos attributed to the Lord after the fact. God had repeatedly identified these as the consequences for Israel of disobeying the covenant they made with Him at Mount Sinai. Look at the following passages and compare their predictions with Amos's fulfillment: Leviticus 26:14–39; Deuteronomy 28:15–46; 1 Kings 8:33–40.

What form of correction remained in store for Israel after refusing all of the previous chastening by the Lord? (Amos 4:12, 13)

According to the following topics, what is revealed in Amos 5:1–15 about the lamentation of Amos over the impending judgment of God on Israel?

Severity (vv. 1–3)

Possible avoidance (vv. 4–7, 14, 15)

The Judge (vv. 8, 9)

Injustice (vv. 10–13)

BEHIND THE SCENES

Justice and righteousness (Amos 5:7) are two of the most important concepts in the prophets. Righteousness is the quality of life demonstrated by those who live up to the established norms in a relationship. They "do right by" another person. Justice is the judicial process of determining who is right in a case of law. The just party was helped by the court. Amos's contention is that the poor are not being defended in the court. Therefore, justice is not done.[5]

BEHIND THE SCENES

Judgment could be averted if God were sought. But seeking God would be altogether different from even enthusiastically observing the rites of worship at the sanctuaries at Bethel and Gilgal and at Beersheba. (Beersheba was a place of pilgrimage in Amos's time and a place of worship for Abraham, Isaac, and Jacob years earlier.) It was expected that God could be found at the sanctuaries, but the priests seem to have offered "life" through religious offerings without stressing the kind of living required from those who truly seek God. (See also 5:6, 14, 24; Ps. 27:8.)[6]

Amos stresses that righteousness and justice are essential to a healthy society. Religion is more than observing feast days and holding sacred assemblies; true religion demands righteous living. The way a man treats his neighbor reveals his relationship with God.[7]

In his first song of woe over Israel (Amos 5:16–27), how did Amos describe the following?

The future day of the Lord (vv. 16–20)

Israel's current religious festivals (vv. 21–24)

Israel's past faithlessness (vv. 25–27)

BIBLE EXTRA

Restoration and the Futility of Religious Ritual
(Amos 5:21–23). Because man consistently has thought to
earn God's acceptance by his own performance, men came
to think even of their spiritual relationship with God only in
terms of externals. They thought that just by observing certain
rules and regulations, performing certain rituals, and speaking
certain words, they could stay in favor with God.

The Lord set them straight concerning this misconcep-
tion in the words of the prophets. He let them know that He
despised their ritualistic worship and empty sacrifices (Amos
5:21, 22), mock solemnity (Is. 58:4, 5), and lip-service devotion (Jer. 7:4). He had become sick of their singing, in which
they only mouthed deceptive words that meant nothing to
them (Amos 5:23). He vowed to turn their singing into wailing
and cause their songs to become songs of lamentation and
mourning (Jer. 7:34).[8]

In his second song of woe (Amos 6:1–14), how did Amos
denounce the materialism of Israel in each of these paragraphs?

6:1, 2

6:3–7

6:8–11

6:12–14

 FAITH ALIVE

We also are living in a prosperous, materialistic society.
Because we are prosperous, we may deceive ourselves into
believing that we have God's blessing on us. The tendency to
give God material goods and believe we have satisfied Him is

ever with us. Material prosperity often leads to religious and moral corruption. Observation of external rites is not enough. God demands our obedience—a heartfelt attitude that issues an action to meet the needs of our fellow human beings.[9]

In what areas of life do you sense that you need to guard against materialism making you insensitive to the Lord and to needy people?

What opportunities do you have through your church and Christian agencies to share your material goods with people in need?

What is one practical step that you could take to become more involved in responding to the material and spiritual needs of poor people in your community?

INJUSTICE IS REMEDIED BY JUDGMENT

The cruel injustice of the northern kingdom of Israel had reached such a state in the days of Amos that judgment was certain. The final three chapters of the Book of Amos contain five visions given the prophet about the coming judgment. In the first vision and in the final message of hope, you see the merciful heart of God ever reaching out in love to His stubborn and faithless people.

In the first vision of judgment given to Amos (7:1–3), what was revealed about each of these subjects?

The nature of the day of the Lord

The intercession of Amos

In the second vision of judgment given to Amos (7:4–6), what was added to the revelation of the first vision about these subjects?

The nature of the day of the Lord

The intercession of Amos

Visions three and four differ from the first two visions in that the Lord asked Amos what he saw and then explained the symbolism of the object relative to the imminent judgment of Israel. Explain the third vision (7:7–9) according to these topics.

The purpose of a plumb line

The nature of a wall built with a plumb line

The role of the plumb line in testing Israel

The outcome of the test of Israel

    KINGDOM EXTRA

Steps to Knowing God and His Ways (Amos 7:7–9). God's judgments should never be a complete surprise because we already know what His standards are. His Word (both the Scriptures and also as incarnate in the Lord Jesus Christ) will announce beforehand any judgment to give His people ample opportunity to repent and turn from their sin (see 2 Chr. 7:14).

Develop an ear to hear what the Spirit is saying (through the prophets) to the churches. Know that God judges everyone equally by the standards of His Word and by the life of Jesus Christ.[10]

Explain the interchange between Amaziah the priest of Bethel and Amos according to these topics.

Amaziah's complaint against Amos

Amos's defense of his ministry

Amos's prediction about Amaziah

How Amaziah represented all of Israel

Explain the prophetic significance of Amos's fourth vision (8:1–3) according to these topics.

How the basket of summer fruit pictured readiness for judgment

How a basket of summer fruit pictured the end of God's patience

How a basket of summer fruit could suggest corpses strewn around

Amos 8:4–14 is the prophet's direct and vivid description of the day of the Lord. Summarize it according to these topics.

The attitudes of the cruel and unjust (vv. 4–6)

The motivation of the Lord's judgment (vv. 7, 8)

The terrors of the day of the Lord (vv. 9, 10)

The immediate result of the judgment (vv. 11–14)

The fifth vision of Amos (9:1–10) differs from the other four because it is a vision of the Lord. The focus is not on what Amos saw but on what he heard the Lord say during the vision. In this way the Lord Himself explained the necessity of judgment on unjust Israel. What did the Lord say about His judgment in terms of these topics?

The false worship centers (v. 1)

His pursuit of the cruelly unjust (vv. 2–4)

His sovereign power (vv. 5, 6)

Judgment as sifting (vv. 7–10)

The book of Amos ends with a hopeful note of restoration. Tell how each of these concluding passages addresses the correction of a former injustice.

Amos 9:11 corrects 9:1

Amos 9:12 corrects 1:3—2:3

Amos 9:13–15 corrects 4:6–11

FAITH ALIVE

God is incredibly longsuffering with our sinful ways, as He was with the nation of Israel. What do you think triggers God's decision to begin chastening us as His beloved children?

If we resent the chastening of the Lord in response to our sinfulness, how does our resentment affect the chastisement?

Amos makes clear that, for God, righteousness and justice go far beyond "doing church" in ways that are, for us, comforting, even exciting, and "with the culture" in methods and styles of worship and communication. Righteousness and justice are dimensions of God's will for how a community lives together, how the strong relate to the weak, the rich to the poor, and so forth. They are dimensions of His kingdom's coming on earth, among people.

Take time to evaluate your participation in your church: At what points may your worship celebrate only your own privilege instead of celebrating God and His provision—and then channeling it through ministry in Christ's name to your community beyond your church?

Ask yourself and God, What are places in our local community where we the body of Christ can minister not only in words that communicate the gospel, but also in deeds that manifest Amos-like righteousness and justice? (Of course, these two are not distinct options, but we, like Amos's hearers, easily deceive ourselves into thinking that our concern for one automatically takes care of the other.)

1. *Spirit-Filled Life Bible* (Nashville: Thomas Nelson Publishers, 1991), 1286, "Introduction: Literary Features."

2. Ibid., "Truth-in-Action through Amos."

3. Ibid., 1291, note on Amos 3:2.

4. Ibid., 1292, note on Amos 4:1.

5. Ibid., 1294, note on Amos 5:7.

6. Ibid., 1293, note on Amos 5:4.

7. Ibid., 1286, "Amos: Introduction, Personal Application."

8. Ibid., 2014, "The Holy Spirit and Restoration: The Futility of Religious Ritual."

9. Ibid., 1286, "Amos: Introduction, Personal Application."

10. Ibid., 1301, " Truth-in-Action through Amos."

Lesson 6/The Truth About Opposing God
Obadiah and Nahum 1—3

In gold and red letters against a dark green background, the "message" T-shirts of the college student strolling across campus pitted two statements against one another. The top one said, "God Is Dead—Nietzsche," while the bottom one proclaimed, "Nietzsche Is Dead—God."

In the latter half of the nineteenth century, Friedrich Nietzsche (*nee*-chee) was an influential philosopher who had a great deal to say about the demise of serious, rugged theism under the gentle influences of Christianity. For a century now, nothing more has been heard from Nietzsche. God, however, continues to make Himself known to people of faith all around the globe.

WHAT GOES AROUND COMES AROUND

The prophets Obadiah and Nahum addressed their prophecies against nations that opposed God and His people. Like Nietzsche, they mocked God. As in Nietzsche's case, God also had the last word against these opponents. Obadiah addressed his prophecy, the shortest book in the Old Testament, against the nation of Edom.

 BIBLE EXTRA

Look up the following Old Testament passages in order to learn more about the identity of Edom and its relationship with the people of Israel.

Genesis 25:21–28; Genesis 36:1

Genesis 35:23—36:43

Numbers 20:14–21

2 Samuel 8:13, 14

1 Kings 9:26–28

2 Kings 8:16, 20–22

Why did the Lord send a harsh message of judgment against Edom by the prophet Obadiah? (Obad. 10–14)

 BEHIND THE SCENES

The date of the prophecy of Obadiah is not definite. Many biblical commentators think that the attack on Jerusalem occurred in the reign of Jehoram (2 Kin. 8:20–22) much earlier than the Babylonian destruction of Jerusalem. However, other biblical authors identify the Edomites as particularly guilty allies of the Babylonians in the destruction of Jerusalem in 586 B.C. (see Ps. 137; Ezek. 25:12–14; 35:1–15).

What was the vision of Obadiah about Edom? (Obad. 1, 2)

What was the basic sin of Edom, and how severe was it? (Obad. 3, 4)

FAITH ALIVE

Steps to Knowing God and His Ways (Obad. 4). God hates pride. It is pride to believe we are invulnerable and to place our trust in any other than God. He will humble those who exalt themselves in this way.

Exalt God. Glorify Him for the security and success you experience. Refuse to judge others, knowing that any judgment or criticism you pass may return to you. Do not rejoice in judgment on others.[1]

Describe the thoroughness of the destruction of Edom promised by the Lord through the vision of Obadiah. (Obad. 5–9)

What fate awaits all the nations on the day of the Lord? (Obad. 15, 16)

What fate awaits Mount Zion on the day of the Lord? (Obad. 17)

PROBING THE DEPTHS

The "Day of the LORD" in Prophecy (Obad. 15). The "day of the LORD" is a term used by the Old Testament prophets to signify a time in the history of mankind when God directly intervenes to bring salvation to His people and punishment to the rebellious. By it God restores His righteous order to the Earth. The terms "that Day" and simply "the Day" are sometimes used as synonyms for the fuller expression "the day of the LORD." The fulfillment of the Day may be seen in four different ways:

1) In the times of the prophets it was revealed by such events as the invasion of Israel by foreign powers (Amos), the awesome plagues of locusts (Joel), and the return of Israelite exiles from captivity (Ezra and Nehemiah).

2) In that prophetic insight had the quality of merging periods of eschatology so that even the prophets themselves could not always distinguish the various times of the fulfillments of their prophecies, that Day developed into a broad biblical concept. Prophetic fulfillments closest to the prophets' own days were mingled with those reaching as far as the final culmination of all things. Hence, the First Coming of Christ and the church age began another phase of the Day of the Lord. As participants in this aspect of the Day, the church can call on the risen Christ to cast down forces that hinder God's work in this present world and to bring about innumerable blessings. This is clear in comparing Isaiah 61:1, 2 with Luke 4:18, 19 and Joel 2:28–32 with Acts 2:16–21.

3) The Second Coming of Christ will inaugurate the third aspect of the day of the Lord, during which Christ's righteous and universal rule will restore God's order to Earth (Amos 9:13; Is. 11:6–9).

4) The ultimate fulfillment of the day of the Lord awaits the full arrival of the world to come, with its new heaven and new earth. Compare Ezekiel 47:1–12 with Revelation 22:1–5.[2]

According to Obadiah's final message of hope, what fate awaits each of the following peoples? (Obad. 17–21)

The house of Jacob (the southern kingdom of Judah)

The house of Joseph (the northern kingdom of Israel)

Edom

Other surrounding nations

 FAITH ALIVE

What do you think is the relationship between pride and the desire to see people close to you fail?

Who close to you are you tempted to treat with disdain or unforgiveness as Edom treated Judah?

How can you realistically alter your attitude and your actions toward this person?

If you allow resentment and bitterness toward another person to grow unchecked, how can you expect your attitudes to "come around" and have a negative impact on your life?

 ## FAITH ALIVE

The godly person does not rejoice in the destruction of God's people, but, like God, he seeks their reconciliation to God and their restoration to holiness and blessing. He avoids pride and the deception it produces in human hearts. Ask God to reveal any areas in which your heart is deceived because of pride. Receive the reconciliation and restoration that come through repentence.[3]

SEPARATING SHEEP FROM GOATS

Nahum addressed his prophecy against the Assyrian Empire that had conquered and deported the northern kingdom of Israel in 722 B.C. (see 2 Kings 17:5, 6, 24). One hundred and ten years later the Assyrians faced conquest as the Babylonians, in league with the Medes and Scythians, prepared to conquer Nineveh, the Assyrian capital city. Nahum assured the people of God that the Lord would show His mercy to them by judging those who oppressed them.

BEHIND THE SCENES

Nahum's message is the only prophecy in the Old Testament identified as a book (Nah. 1:1). Nineveh, representing the entire Assyrian Empire, was a magnificent city located on the eastern bank of the Tigris River in modern Iraq. It was founded by Nimrod (Gen. 10:8–11) and was surrounded by a wall almost eight miles in circumference. The city could accommodate an estimated 300,000 people.[4]

What is the effect of each of the following qualities of the Lord upon His enemies (the goats)? (Nah. 1:2, 3a)

His jealousy

His fury

His slow anger

What is the effect of each of the following qualities of the Lord upon His friends (the sheep)? (Nah. 1:7, 15)

His goodness

His protectiveness

His revelation of good news

 KINGDOM EXTRA

Key Lessons in Faith (Nah. 1:7, 15). A key test of faith for God's people comes when God judges the nations around them. For Christians, this can mean that God may judge the nation in which they live. He is able to protect and spare His people from judgment that falls even on their neighbors.

Trust that: (a) God is good! (b) He is a place of safety for us when we are in trouble. (c) He is faithful to care for those who trust Him to do so. Believe that God is willing and able to deliver us from any bondage. Know that He will eventually stop any attack upon us. Hear and believe the good news of deliverance from our soul's enemy through Jesus Christ.[5]

   WORD WEALTH

Peace (Nah. 1:15), *shalom. Shalom* comes from the root verb *shalam,* meaning "to be complete, perfect, and full." Thus *shalom* is much more than the absence of war and conflict; it is the wholeness that the entire human race seeks.

The word *shalom* occurs about 250 times in the Old Testament. In Psalm 35:27, God takes delight in the *shalom* (the wholeness, the total well-being) of His servant. In Isaiah 53:5 the chastisement necessary to bring us *shalom* was upon the suffering Messiah. The angels understood at His birth that Jesus was to be the great peace-bringer, as they called out, "Glory to God in the highest: and on earth peace, goodwill toward men!" (Luke 2:14–17; compare Is. 9:7).[6]

What does the power of God as shown in nature suggest about the judgment of God on wicked people? (Nah. 1:3b–6)

What will become of the best plans of the enemies of the Lord? (Nah. 1:9–11)

   BEHIND THE SCENES

"The one who plots evil" (Nah. 1:11) is probably a general reference to the habitually wicked character of the Assyrian rulers. It could either refer to Sennacherib, whose planned attack on Jerusalem in 701 B.C. was thwarted (2 Kin. 18), or to Ashurbanipal, the last great Assyrian ruler (669–627 B.C.), who conquered Egypt and forced King Manasseh of Judah to submit as his puppet (2 Chr. 33:11–13).[7]

What will become of those oppressed by the best plans of the enemies of the Lord? (Nah. 1:12, 13)

What was the command of the Lord concerning Assyria? (Nah. 1:14)

     FAITH ALIVE

How have you observed the unrighteous reap the results of their rebellion and the people of God receive His goodness and protection?

What consolation do you gain from knowing that the anger of the Lord is slow? (Nah. 1:3)

THE BIGGER THEY ARE, THE HARDER THEY FALL

The final two chapters of Nahum contain one of the most vivid poetic descriptions of an ancient battle. Take heed, the prophet warned: no one, no matter how mighty, is strong enough to box with God. His opponents will go down without mercy.

According to the following topics, describe the attack on Nineveh by the armies of Babylon, Media, and Scythia. (Nah. 2:1, 3–6)

The siege (v. 1)

The attackers (vv. 3, 4)

The defenders (v. 5)

The surprise attack (v. 6)

BEHIND THE SCENES

"He who scatters" (Nah. 2:1) is the coalition of Babylonians, Medes, and Scythians about to attack Nineveh. The Assyrians practiced a policy of deporting conquered peoples from their homelands and scattering them throughout their empire, thereby stripping them of identity and continuity. The tribes of the northern kingdom suffered this fate. But Assyria the great scatterer will be scattered by others.[8]

BEHIND THE SCENES

Besides the Tigris River on the west, the Khoser, a spring-fed stream, traversed Nineveh. A canal also ran through the city. Sennacherib (705–681 B.C.) had built a series of dams to control water flow. The invaders likely closed the gates of the river to stop the flow of water and make their approach to Nineveh easier, then suddenly opened the gates (Nah. 2:6) to release torrents of water and unleash a destructive flood on the city. The palace, likely constructed of dried mud bricks, would literally dissolve.[9]

What was on the Lord's mind while the judgment of Assyria progressed? (Nah. 2:2)

According to the following topics, describe the defeat of Nineveh by the armies of Babylonia, Media, and Scythia. (Nah. 2:7–13)

The decreed fate (v. 7)

The flight (vv. 8, 10)

The plunder (v. 9)

The lion, national symbol of Assyria (vv. 11, 12)

The outcome (v. 13)

What were the sins of Nineveh for which God would destroy her? (Nah. 3:1–4)

How do you think the sins of Nineveh made her like a prostitute? (Nah. 3:4)

How was the destruction of Nineveh like the public humiliation of a prostitute? (Nah. 3:5–7)

 BEHIND THE SCENES

Nahum 3:8–11 compares the fall of Nineveh to the fall of No Amon in Egypt. Amon was the supreme sun-god of Egypt. No Amon, meaning "City of Amon," was also known as Thebes. Thebes, located on the upper Nile River about 350 miles south of modern Cairo, was the center of the Egyptian Empire for nearly 1,400 years, until Assyria conquered it in 663 B.C. It was surrounded by waterways and sacred temples, much like Nineveh, and boasted allies like Put (Somaliland) and Lubim (Libya). The greatness of Thebes was legendary. Nahum mentioned her as a reminder that even the greatest fall.[10]

The defenses of Nineveh were no match for the armies sent by the Lord as His agents of judgment on Assyria. How did the prophet Nahum belittle each of the following aspects of the defense system of Nineveh? (Nah. 3:12–19)

The forts (v. 12)

The populace (v. 13)

The dependence on water and clay (vv. 14, 15a)

The army and its leaders (vv. 15b–17)

The king and his advisers (vv. 18, 19)

 FAITH ALIVE

What contemporary opponents of our faith seem to you to be too powerful to overcome in human strength?

How could the prophecy of Nahum affect you in each of the following areas when you consider people, organizations, or cultural trends that oppose God?

Attitude toward the future

Courage

Prayer life

Witnessing

Write out Ephesians 6:12.

What does this verse remind us to keep in mind with regard to our "enemies"?

What does Ephesians 6:13–18 tell us we are to do as we overcome spiritual opposition around us?

v. 13

v. 14

v. 15

v. 16

v. 17

v. 18

1. *Spirit-Filled Life Bible* (Nashville: Thomas Nelson Publishers, 1991), 1308, "Truth-in-Action through Obadiah."
2. Ibid., 1306–1307, "Kingdom Dynamics: Obad. 10 The 'Day of the LORD' in Prophecy."
3. Ibid., 1308, "Truth-in-Action through Obadiah."
4. Ibid., 1333, note on Nahum 1:1.
5. Ibid., 1337, "Truth-in-Action through Nahum."
6. Ibid., 1334, "Word Wealth: Nahum 1:15 peace."
7. Ibid., note on Nahum 1:11.
8. Ibid., 1334–1335, note on Nahum 2:1.
9. Ibid., 1335, note on Nahum 2:6.
10. Ibid., 1336, note on Nahum 3:8, 9.

Lesson 7/The Truth About Crossing Cultures
Jonah 1—4

He grew up in the Midwest, and he had been to Canada a few times. He lived in Texas for a while and saw some border towns in Mexico. But the trip to Guatemala to see his missionary sister was his first real prolonged encounter with a distinct culture. Just how distinct first showed itself in the Pan Am concourse at Miami International Airport.

The flight was late arriving from New York, and none of the other waiting passengers milling around spoke English. Among the travelers were a half dozen young people dressed for the nightclub scene. They ignored everyone else, going to the front of any line, breaking into any conversation with airline officials when they wanted to.

Later in Guatemala City the traffic surprised the traveler. Streets were jammed with trucks, buses, and taxis that shared a common disdain for traffic signals and speed limits. The air smelled of diesel fumes, and black exhaust smoke choked the streets. The food surprised him more than the traffic. He had expected the food to be spicy like Mexican dishes, but it was bland.

In the village where his sister lived, work dominated life. By dawn the Indian women and children were cutting broccoli on a large farm for fifty cents a day and the men were working the terraced corn fields on the sides of the mountain. Signs of deforestation showed, even though the fence posts and utility poles were made of concrete containing volcanic ash.

When his sister left him with her truck in the middle of the village while she did some business, a crowd of young

Indian men gathered just to look at him. They pointed and talked animatedly. In time they laughed at him. Then the laughter became hilarious. Someone called out to him in the local dialect, and when he smiled the crowd again roared with laughter. He wondered if he were in any danger. He had never felt so alone, so useless, so out of place.

CROSSING CULTURES ON BUSINESS

A casual glance at the Book of Jonah shows that the prophet was not uncomfortable among Gentiles. He readily traveled and interacted with them. Jonah could talk about spiritual matters with Gentiles without discomfort (Jon. 1:9, 10). But Jonah was dead set against one group of Gentiles—the Assyrians. He did not want them to be the recipient of God's mercy. God was opposed to that attitude on Jonah's part and set out to change it.

 ## BEHIND THE SCENES

As indicated in 2 Kings 14:25, Jonah was the son of Amittai and a native of Gath Hepher, a village three miles northeast of Nazareth, within the tribal borders of Zebulun. Prophesying during the reign of Jeroboam II and immediately preceding Amos, he was a strong nationalist who was fully aware of the havoc the Assyrians had wrought in Israel over the years. Jonah found it difficult to accept the fact that God would offer mercy to Nineveh of Assyria when its inhabitants deserved severe punishment.

He was the only prophet sent to preach to the Gentiles. Elijah was sent to Sarepta to live for a season (1 Kin. 17:8–10) and Elisha journeyed to Damascus (2 Kin. 8:7), but only Jonah was given a message . . . to preach directly to a Gentile city. His reluctance to preach at Nineveh was based upon a desire to see their decline culminate in a complete loss of power. Also he feared that God would show mercy, thus extending the Assyrians' opportunity to harass Israel.[1]

What was the commission of the Lord to Jonah, and what was its motivation? (Jon. 1:1, 2)

What was the response of Jonah to the Lord's commission, and what was his motivation? (Jon. 1:3; 4:2)

 BEHIND THE SCENES

Tarshish (Jon. 1:3) is considered by most to be Tartessus on the coast of southwestern Spain. As such it represents a distant place where God had not revealed Himself. Jonah is trying to escape "the presence of the LORD." This indicates that he had a very localized view of God's presence or perhaps a belief that the Spirit of prophecy could not follow him there. He begins his voyage at the port city of Joppa, about thirty-five miles northwest of Jerusalem, a seaport for Israel.[2]

Jonah 1:4–16 is a carefully arranged literary unit centered on verses 9 and 10. Notice the balance of this section by observing the following pairs of passages.

How does Jonah 1:15, 16 complete the thought begun in 1:4, 5a?

How does Jonah 1:13, 14 balance the events in 1:5b, 6?

How does Jonah 1:12 respond to 1:6?

How does Jonah 1:11 correspond to 1:8?

How do Jonah 1:9 and 10 form the heart of this narrative?

KINGDOM EXTRA

Understanding sin (Jon. 1:4–15). God cannot allow known sin to remain unconfronted in the lives of any who love and serve Him. Because sin cannot stand in the presence of God's holiness, prayer is vain and useless until confession of sin removes the spiritual barrier we have constructed between ourselves and Him.

Confront sin in your life. Readily confess any wrong-doing. Remember that you cannot hide from God.[3]

Describe Jonah's interaction with the pagan mariners in chapter one according to these topics.

His attitude toward them

His willingness to talk about spiritual issues

His witness to the power of God

His interest in the safety of the sailors

FAITH ALIVE

How do regular working contacts with people of other ethnic groups tend to reduce barriers between races?

Why is it easier to talk about spiritual topics with people of different backgrounds after you have first struggled together with difficulties?

What does Jonah 1 suggest to you as some ways to reduce tensions between ethnic groups?

GRATITUDE FOR PERSONAL FORGIVENESS

The spiritual dilemma for Jonah, caused by God's commissioning him to preach to the residents of Nineveh, revolved around the mercy of God. Jonah did not want God to show mercy to the Assyrians of Nineveh, who were threatening Jonah's country, the northern kingdom of Israel. At the same time that Jonah did not want Nineveh to know the mercy of God, he himself was delighted to experience it in the depths of the sea!

What was the purpose of the "great fish" in the plans of God for Jonah? (Jon. 1:17; 2:10)

How did Jonah describe his prayer from the belly of the great fish? (Jon. 2:2, 7)

How did Jonah understand his experience in the belly of the great fish? (Jon. 2:3–6)

 BIBLE EXTRA

In the Gospels Jesus spoke about "the sign of the prophet Jonah" (Matt. 12:38–42; 16:1–4; Luke 11:29–32). The key to understanding how Jonah functioned as a sign in the ministry of Jesus is found in Matthew 12:40. According to that verse, what was "the sign of the prophet Jonah"?

What else was spiritually significant from Jonah's story for the Israelites of Jesus' day? (Matt. 12:41; Luke 11:32)

What did Jonah conclude about the mercy of God while he was in the belly of the great fish? (Jon. 2:8, 9)

What are the implications of the truth that Jonah learned about the mercy of God (Jon. 2:8, 9) for his reluctance to proclaim judgment on Nineveh? (see Jon. 4:2)

 FAITH ALIVE

Why might a close encounter with death cause a Christian to rethink his or her animosity toward another ethnic, religious, or other minority group?

How might a renewed sense of personal unworthiness to receive the mercy of God cause the same thing?

CROSSING CULTURES WITH A MESSAGE

Jonah went to Nineveh and proclaimed a message of imminent destruction. In all likelihood, Jonah didn't hold out a particle of hope to the residents of the Assyrian capital. He certainly did not make any suggestions about ways to avoid the judgment of God. He was quite literally a prophet of doom.

According to Jonah 3:1–4, summarize each of these topics.

The directive of the Lord (vv. 1, 2)

The response of Jonah (v. 3)

The message of Jonah (v. 4)

Contrast Jonah's response to the Lord in Jonah 1:1–3 and 3:1–4.

BEHIND THE SCENES

The expression "Nineveh was an exceedingly great city, a three-day journey in extent" (Jon. 3:3) seems to indicate that Jonah preached to an area we might today call Greater Nineveh. In Genesis 10:11, 12, Nimrod's five cities centered upon Nineveh are identified with the same Hebrew words translated "an exceedingly great city" in Jonah 1:2; 3:2; and 4:11. It would have taken three days to walk across that territory and many more days to cover it on a preaching tour.[4]

What was the reaction in Greater Nineveh to the proclamation of imminent doom by the prophet Jonah?

By the populace (Jon. 3:5)

By the king (Jon. 3:6, 7)

What insight into God and the moral order of His creation is revealed in the decree of the king and nobility of Nineveh? (Jon. 3:7–9)

How did the repentance of the Ninevites in response to Jonah's preaching compare with the repentance of the northern kingdom of Israel to the preaching of Jonah and the other prophets?

Do you think God's nature required Him to be merciful to the residents of Greater Nineveh, or was His decision to spare them an act He could have left undone without calling His mercy into question? Why do you think so?

FAITH ALIVE

What would you think of a missionary who went to another culture with the attitudes toward it that Jonah took to Nineveh? (See Jon. 4:1, 2.)

What mixed feelings would you have if you saw someone you intensely disliked repent of sin and turn to God?

What mixed feelings do you have about the sincerity or effectiveness of the worship of other ethnic or religious groups?

ANGER FOR CROSS-CULTURAL FORGIVENESS

Jonah's miraculous encounter with the wonderful mercy of God had not prepared him to rejoice when the dreaded enemies of his country experienced that transforming mercy. He did not want Nineveh to survive to be the instrument of judgment in the hand of God against his spiritually rebellious fellow countrymen. His national loyalties overpowered his spiritual loyalties.

Contrast the response of the Ninevites to the plan of the Lord (Jon. 3:5, 6) with Jonah's reaction to His plan. (4:1)

Contrast the proclamation of the king of Nineveh (Jon. 3:7–9) with the prayer of Jonah (4:2, 3).

How did God show mercy both to the Ninevites (Jon. 3:10) and to Jonah (4:4)?

FAITH ALIVE

Knowing God and His Ways (Jon. 4:1–11). God's prevailing self-revelation is His love, graciousness, forgiveness, and mercy. We must allow this knowledge of God's nature to shape our character accordingly.

Never underestimate the Lord's mercy and His willingness to forgive. Never discourage repentance, nor be grieved when an enemy decides to repent and escape the judgment you may feel he deserves.[5]

Why do you think Jonah set up his shelter and kept vigil over Nineveh? (Jon. 4:5)

How did God extend His mercy to Jonah through the three things He "prepared" for him? (Jon. 1:17; 4:6, 7)

What do you think Jonah revealed about himself by his repeated wishes to die? (Jon. 4:3, 8, 9)

What do you think God wanted Jonah to realize in response to His repeated question, "Is it right for you to be angry?" (Jon. 4:4, 9)

Explain the irony of Jonah's compassion for the plant and hatred for Nineveh. (Jon. 4:9, 10)

What lessons should Jonah have learned from his experience with the plant, the worm, and the oppressive sun? (Jon. 4:6–11)

About himself

About God

FAITH ALIVE

What do you think racial hatred among Christians reveals about their spiritual maturity?

What do the following Scriptures mandate regarding the unity of races within the body of Christ?

Acts 17:26

1 Cor. 12:12

Gal. 3:26–28

James 2:1–9

What does the Book of Jonah suggest about the kind of approach God would take to change the racial attitudes of one of His children?

1. *Spirit-Filled Life Bible* (Nashville: Thomas Nelson Publishers, 1991), 1309, "Jonah: Introduction."
2. Ibid., 1312, note on Jonah 1:3.
3. Ibid., 1315, "Truth-in-Action through Jonah."
4. T. Desmond Alexander, "Jonah," from *Obadiah, Jonah, Micah: An Introduction and Commentary* (Downers Grove: Inter-Varsity Press, 1988), 57–58.
5. *Spirit-Filled Life Bible*, 1315, "Truth-in-Action through Jonah."

Lesson 8/The Truth About the Majesty of God
Micah 1—8

Recently United Airlines aired a stunning television commercial filled with idyllic images of English scenery and people. Behind the pictures but in front of the airline musical signature, a rich voice intoned an edited version of these lines from *Richard II.*

> This royal throne of kings, this sceptered isle,
> This earth of majesty, this seat of Mars,
> This other Eden, demi-Paradise,
> This fortress built by Nature for herself
> Against infection and the hand of war,
> This happy breed of men, this little world,
> This precious stone set in the silver sea,
> Which serves it in the office of a wall
> Or as a moat defensive to a house
> Against the envy of less happier lands—
> This blessed plot, this earth, this realm, this
>   England.[1]

The airline advertisement had a tone of majesty to it because the words are glorious. Shakespeare wanted to impart to England a sense of dignity, grandeur, stateliness, and authority. He did it by praising England for her warrior kings, her scenic beauty, and her splendid island isolation.

When the prophet Micah wanted to praise the Lord, the God of Israel, he rifled the Hebrew language to find the poetry to extol the dignity, grandeur, stateliness, and authority of "the majesty of the name of the Lord our God" (Mic. 5:4). Micah followed Isaiah in warning the southern kingdom of

Judah of impending judgment if the nation did not repent. Later, Jeremiah knew Micah's prophesies and even quoted him by name (Jer. 26:18; Mic. 3:12).

GOD THE JUDGE

Micah pronounced judgment on Judah as Amos had done in Israel fifty years earlier. Micah's prophecies contain much more hope for future restoration than did Amos's because of the focus on the person of the majestic Lord. However, Micah began with God as the Judge calling His rebellious people into court to answer for their sins.

What is the verbal clue in Micah 1:2; 3:1; and 6:1 that major divisions of the book begin at these points?

What do these verses also tell readers about the character of the Book of Micah?

Describe the following aspects of the courtroom scene in Micah 1:2–7.

The defendants (v. 2)

The witness (v. 2)

The arrival of the Judge (vv. 2–4)

The occasion (v. 5)

The sentence (vv. 6, 7)

BEHIND THE SCENES

In 722 B.C. the Assyrian Empire carried out the sentence pronounced in Micah 1:6, 7 upon Samaria and the northern kingdom of Israel. In the same military campaign, Assyria defeated the armies of Egypt and conquered all of the fortresses guarding the approaches to Jerusalem before the Lord miraculously destroyed the Assyrian army as it besieged Jerusalem (2 Kin. 18; 19). Micah 1:8–16 recounts the mourning of the prophet over the Judean cities destroyed by the Assyrians advancing on Jerusalem. One of them was Micah's hometown, Moresheth Gath (v. 14).

Describe the reaction of Micah to the suffering of his fellow countrymen at the hands of the Assyrian invaders. (Mic. 1:8, 9)

What reaction did the prophet expect from his fellow countrymen when they heard of the devastation caused by the Assyrians? (Mic. 1:16)

BIBLE EXTRA

Look up the following Old Testament references and record what each one reveals about the customs of mourning in Israelite culture.

Genesis 50:7–10

Jeremiah 6:26

Ezekiel 24:15–18 (here the normal customs are forbidden)

How did Micah use the meaning of the name of each of the following Judean towns to highlight the distress that came on God's rebellious people?

Beth Aphrah [House of Dust] (1:10)

Shaphir [Beautiful Town] (1:11)

Zaanan [Going-Out Town] (1:11)

Beth Ezel [House of Taking Away] (1:11)

Maroth [Bitter Town] (1:12)

Lachish [sounds like "To the Steeds"] (1:13)

Moresheth [Possession Town] (1:14)

Achzib [Deception Town] (1:14)

Mareshah [Inheritance Town] (1:15)

According to the following topics, describe the message which the Lord as Judge pronounced against oppressive landowners. (Mic. 2:1–5)

Their offense (vv. 1, 2)

Their sentence (vv. 3–5)

According to the following topics, describe the message which the Lord as Judge pronounced against lying prophets. (Mic. 2:6–11)

Their reaction to true prophets (v. 6)

The value of true prophets (v. 7)

The offense of the false prophets (vv. 8, 9)

The fate of the false prophets (vv. 10, 11)

FAITH ALIVE

Keys to Wise Living (Mic. 2:6, 7, 11). Wisdom teaches us to accept God's assessment of man, as difficult as it may be due to our humanistic milieu. Be warned that only listening to what we want to hear will breed disobedience and ungodliness.

Never discourage leaders from speaking the whole counsel of God. Do not reprove teachers and preachers for speaking correction or warning. Refuse to listen to God's Word selectively. Receive the correction as well as the affirmation.[2]

According to the following topics, describe the Lord's deliverance of Jerusalem by the Lord, the awesome Judge, from the besieging Assyrians. (Mic. 2:12, 13; see 2 Kin. 19:31–34, esp. v. 31)

The awesome Judge's role in the siege (v. 12)

The divine deliverance (v. 13)

FAITH ALIVE

What happens when indifferent Christians, like the false prophets, ignore God, the awesome Judge?

What happens when insecure Christians live in continual, irrational fear of God, the awesome Judge?

In your life, how do you think the experience of God's purifying judgment could strengthen your spiritual life?

THE GLORIOUS KING

Micah 2 ends with the picture of the Lord marching out of liberated Jerusalem ahead of the human king of Judah. In chapters three through five of Micah, the Lord concerns Himself with the leadership of His people. First He critically examines the deficiencies of current leadership. Then He looks ahead to the glories of the Messiah as King of kings.

How did the Lord evaluate the political leaders of His people? (Mic. 3:1–4)

How did the Lord evaluate the spiritual leaders of His people? (Mic. 3:5–7)

What was the irony of the uselessness of the prophets of Judah? (Mic. 3:8)

BEHIND THE SCENES

[This] outstanding reference to the Spirit of God (Mic. 3:8) occurs in Micah's contrast of the authority behind his ministry with that of the counterfeit prophets of his day. While other men were made bold by intoxicants to fabricate tales in the format of prophecies, the true power, might, and justice behind Micah's message came from his anointing "by the Spirit of the LORD."[3]

How did the Lord evaluate the Jerusalem establishment as leaders of the nation? (Mic. 3:9–12)

FAITH ALIVE

Lessons for Leaders (Mic. 3:5–7, 11). Spiritual leadership is a sacred trust. Though often coveted by the spiritual neophyte, it is a costly role for anyone who serves in it. Leaders, believe that God will stop speaking in revelation to leaders who become mercenary in their ministries. Leaders, be warned: never, never set a price on your ministry. Never deceitfully seduce people to become your financial support by using psychological or spiritual manipulation.[4]

BEHIND THE SCENES

In the days of Jeremiah, the false prophets and corrupt priests of Jerusalem attempted to convince the civil authorities to execute the prophet. Jeremiah constantly proclaimed a message of judgment while the mainstream religious establishment promised imminent peace and prosperity. The prophets and priests claimed Jeremiah was guilty of treason.

The civil authorities rejected the petition of the religious establishment on the basis of Micah's earlier similar ministry. Some of the elders of Israel said, "Micah of Moresheth prophesied in the days of Hezekiah king of Judah, and spoke to all the people of Judah, saying, 'Thus says the Lord of hosts:

"Zion shall be plowed like a field,
Jerusalem shall become a heap of ruins,
And the mountain of the temple
Like the bare hills of the forest." '

"Did Hezekiah king of Judah and all Judah ever put him
to death?" (Jer. 26:18, 19a).

According to the following topics, describe the future
glory of Jerusalem in contrast to its ignominy predicted at the
end of Micah 3. (Mic. 4:1–5)

Its prominence (v. 1)

The Lord's activity there (vv. 2, 3)

The nation's reaction to Jerusalem and the Lord (vv. 2–5)

According to the following topics, describe how the Lord
intends to prepare Jerusalem to be a glorious place at the head
of all the earth. (Mic. 4:6—5:5)

The future ideal (4:6–8)

The necessary purification process (4:9, 10)

The arrogance of the nations (4:11, 12)

Jerusalem against the nations (4:13—5:1)

Jerusalem's glorious King (Mic. 5:2–5)

   BIBLE EXTRA

Messiah Born in Bethlehem (Mic. 5:2, 4, 5). Bethlehem
—the name means "House of Bread," and at the "House of
Bread" the Bread of Life was born into the world.

The scribes knew that the Messiah was to be born there. When the wise men inquired about the birth of the new King, the scribes referred to Micah's prophecy (Matt. 2:1–12). Yet none of the theologians bothered to accompany the wise men to see if, indeed, the Messiah had come.

The "little town of Bethlehem" is now a point of pilgrimage for thousands yearly. But let us learn from those who did not make that first pilgrimage: neither our orthodoxy, biblical knowledge, nor religious status guarantees that we will see what God is doing in our midst today. We must be willing to follow the leading of God and His Word if we wish to see the promise fulfilled.[5]

When in the future the Lord's glorious King reigns in Zion, what will Zion's role be? (Mic. 5:5b–9)

Toward Assyria (vv. 5b, 6)

Toward the other nations (vv. 7–9, 15)

What were Jerusalem and all Judah trusting in instead of the Lord and His future glorious King that the Lord needed to purge away from His people? (Mic. 5:10–14)

   FAITH ALIVE

A Step to Holiness (Mic. 5:10–15). Holiness is relying totally upon God's ways and resources and turning from your own. Understand that God will eventually root out any dependence we show upon things that He has not established or way He has not directed.[6]

What maturing process that the Lord is taking you through sometimes feels like the pains of childbirth? Why?

What do you depend on for security that the Lord might need to take away before the glorious King can reign fully in your life?

How has Jesus the glorious King built up and exalted your life since He has become your Savior and Lord?

THE SANCTIFYING SAVIOR

As in the first chapter of Micah's prophecies, chapter six begins with the Lord's calling His people into court to answer His complaint. Before Jerusalem can become the center of the earth, the people of God must face some issues of personal holiness. God, the Judge and glorious King, is also the sanctifying Savior whose majestic holiness can abide no sin.

According to the following topics, describe the courtroom drama the Lord, the sanctifying Savior, initiated against His people. (Mic. 6:1–8)

The legal challenge (vv. 1, 2)

The witnesses (vv. 1, 2)

The Lord's complaint (v. 3)

The Lord's complaint illustrated (vv. 4, 5)

Judah's defense (vv. 6, 7)

The Lord's response to the defense (v. 8)

BEHIND THE SCENES

God was really looking for an ethical response from His Old Covenant people. The rabbis analyzed the Law and found 613 precepts. These were reduced to eleven principles in Psalm 15 and down to six commands in Isaiah 33:15. But here they have been condensed into three: 1) Remain honest in all you do; 2) cherish compassionate faithfulness; and 3) commit yourself to live in submission to your God.[7]

FAITH ALIVE

Understanding Godliness (Mic. 6:8). In its simplest definition, godliness means for us to be overflowing with the fruit of the Spirit. Adopt the four consummate virtues of Christian living: justice, mercy, humility, and faithfulness.[8]

According to the following topics, describe the sentence that the Lord, the sanctifying Savior, pronounced on Judah. (Mic. 6:9–16)

Areas of guilt being punished (vv. 9–12)

Details of the sentence (vv. 13–15)

Why did Micah invoke the memory of Omri and Ahab to describe the iniquity of Judah? (Mic. 6:16; see 1 Kin. 16:30–33)

According to the following topics, describe Micah's assessment of the spiritual condition of Judah. (Mic. 7:1–6)

His search for righteous people (vv. 1, 2)

His rating of leadership (vv. 3, 4)

His findings about the national character (vv. 5, 6)

BEHIND THE SCENES

Jesus indicated that coming persecution against His people could be explained by the words of Micah 7:6 (Matt. 10:35, 36). His emphasis was on the division of families according to how they responded to Him.[9]

What was Micah's resolve after discovering the discouraging nature of Judah's spiritual condition? (Mic. 7:7) What do you think he meant by this statement?

According to the following topics, describe what Micah expected the Lord, the sanctifying Savior, to do while he waited on Him to deal with the iniquity of Judah. (Mic. 7:8–20)

The hope of Jerusalem (vv. 8–10)

The security of Jerusalem (vv. 11–13)

A prayer for Jerusalem and its answer (vv. 14–17)

The hymn of praise by Jerusalem (vv. 18–20)

BEHIND THE SCENES

Micah makes a word play on his own name in 7:18: **Mi** ["who"] **c** ["like"] **ah** ["*Yah*"weh] means "Who Is Like the Lᴏʀᴅ?" or "He Who Is Like Yahweh." The generic name for God ("El," v. 18) is equivalent to the personal name ("Yahweh"). It is not the greatness of God's power that these texts emphasize but His immense compassion and His will to forgive and forget sin in covenant faithfulness to all generations.[10]

FAITH ALIVE

List ways that the Lord sanctifies today:

In His church

In the lives of His children

What sanctifying, purifying work is the Lord doing in you right now?

How is the sanctifying activity of the Lord one of the evidences of His great majesty?

1. William Shakespeare, *Richard II*, II, i, 40–50.

2. *Spirit-Filled Life Bible* (Nashville: Thomas Nelson Publishers, 1991), 1328–1329, "Truth-in-Action through Micah."

3. Ibid., 1318, "Micah: Introduction, The Holy Spirit at Work."

4. Ibid., 1329, "Truth-in-Action through Micah."

5. Ibid., 1324–1325, "Kingdom Dynamics: Micah 5:2, 4, 5 Messiah Born at Bethlehem."

6. Ibid., 1328, "Truth-in-Action through Micah."

7. Ibid., 1326, note on Micah 6:8.

8. Ibid., 1328, "Truth-in-Action through Micah."

9. Ibid., 1327, note on Micah 7:6.

10. Ibid., 1328, note on Micah 7:18–20.

Lesson 9/The Truth About Trusting God
Habakkuk 1—3

Philip Yancey wrote a column for *Christianity Today* in which he explored the way age affects how people remember difficult times. Yancey concluded, "Partly from listening to elderly people, I have learned that faith means trusting in advance what will only make sense in reverse. Fifty years casts another light on a marriage; the century looks different from a ninety-four-year-old view."[1]

Earlier in the article Yancey observed, "Great relationships take form when they are stretched to the breaking point and do not break. . . . Abraham climbing the hill at Moriah, Job scratching his boils in the hot sun, David hiding in a cave, Elijah moping in a desert, Moses pleading for a new job description—all these heroes experienced crisis moments when they were sorely tempted to judge God uncaring, powerless, or even malign. Confused and in the dark, they faced a turning point: whether to turn away embittered, or step forward in faith. In the end, all chose the path of trust, and for this reason we remember them as giants of faith."[2]

To this list of biblical figures facing turning points could be added the prophet Habakkuk staring out from his watchtower. God had confounded Habakkuk with what He intended to do, so the prophet set Him straight and launched his vigil until the Lord came to His senses and changed His mind. The truth about trusting God was hard for Habakkuk to face. How about you?

TRUST IN THE FACE OF DOUBT

The Book of Habakkuk opens with a classic case of getting what you pray for and discovering that the answer wasn't as desirable as you had anticipated. What would Habakkuk do when God's solution seemed much worse than the problem the prophet had prayed about?

How did the prophet describe the message which the Lord had shown him? (Hab. 1:1; see Nah. 1:1; Zech. 9:1; 12:1; Mal. 1:1)

According to the following topics, describe the complaint Habakkuk raised against the Lord. (Hab. 1:2–4)

Habakkuk's prayers (v. 2)

The sins of Judah (vv. 2, 3)

The covenant between God and His people (v. 4)

According to the following topics, describe the response of the Lord to Habakkuk's first complaint. (Hab. 1:5–11)

The general character of His solution (v. 5)

The specific instrument of His judgment (vv. 6, 7)

The warfare of God's instrument (vv. 8–10)

The sin of God's instrument of judgment (v. 11)

According to the following topics, describe Habakkuk's anguished reaction to the Lord's revelation of impending judgment on Judah's sins by means of Babylon. (Hab. 1:12—2:1)

Why Babylon should not be the instrument of judgment on Judah (1:12, 13)

The relative wickedness of Judah and Babylon (1:13)

The immorality of empire-building nations (1:14, 15, 17)

The idolatry of empire-building power (v. 16)

The prophet's challenge to God (2:1)

How did Habakkuk reveal his faith in God by the way he complained to Him, first about the lack of judgment on Judah's sins and then about what seemed excessive and unfair judgment?

What did Habakkuk's vigil on the watchtower say about his faith in God?

 PROBING THE DEPTHS

Habakkuk reminds us that the question "Why?" can, should, and must be asked. His circumstances demanded that he ask God about the apparent reign of unrighteousness around him. Because he believed in God, he believed that God had an answer to his problem. His questions demonstrated the presence of faith, not the lack of it. For an atheist the question "Why?" has no meaning; for a believer the question "Why?" finds its ultimate answer in God.[3]

 FAITH ALIVE

What kinds of doubts do you think may indicate a weak or wavering faith in the Lord?

What kinds of doubts do you think may indicate a strong and active faith in the Lord?

What difficult moment(s) in your life seemed to indicate that the Lord was abandoning you? How did you feel at the time?

How did the situation resolve, and how did the Lord manifest His presence within it?

TRUST IN THE FACE OF MORAL DECAY

The sins of Judah were beyond remedy, and judgment was coming by means of the hopelessly wicked Babylonians. The "cure" would make the disease of wickedness much worse. Would the faith of the prophet endure the moral catastrophe of the Babylonian conquest?

According to the following topics, describe the revelation the Lord finally gave to Habakkuk on his watchtower. (Hab. 2:2, 3)

Its recording (v. 2)

Its time frame (v. 3a)

Its certainty (v. 3b)

 FAITH ALIVE

Steps to Dynamic Devotion (Hab. 2:1–3). God requires that we make our relationship with Him our highest priority, that we bring our deepest questions and turmoils before Him, expecting His answers and guidance. Set aside a regular time and place that is holy to the Lord. Spend time listening for His word as you read, study, and meditate on Scripture. Be faithful in daily prayer.

Document those things the Lord speaks to you or quickens to your heart. Record biblical promises He makes alive to you, and hold fast to them, knowing they will come to pass.[4]

How did the revelation of coming judgment separate the proud Babylonians from the faithful remnant of Judah? (Hab. 2:4, 5)

BEHIND THE SCENES

The evil and arrogant Babylonians are contrasted with the righteous and the trusting among God's people. The transient and unstable nature of one who attempts to find life in himself is compared to the dependability and reliability of one who trusts in God for his life. The Jewish Talmud states: "Moses gave Israel 613 commandments. David reduced them to ten, Isaiah to two, but Habakkuk to one: 'The just shall live by his faith.' "[5]

BIBLE EXTRA

Look up the following three quotations of Habakkuk 2:4 in crucial New Testament passages about salvation and Christian living. Summarize the meaning of each.

Romans 1:16, 17

Galatians 3:10–14

Hebrews 10:35–39 (from the Greek Old Testament)

Paul the apostle takes the statement of Habakkuk 2:4 and makes it the heart of the gospel. The righteousness of God is attained only through faith, so that the right way to live is to trust. Habakkuk calls all believers in all times to trust

God, to be faithful to Him, and so to find life as God means it to be lived. . . .

Also, in Galatians, Paul links the most famous verse in Habakkuk with the reception of the promised Holy Spirit through faith (2:4; Gal. 3:11–14). The righteous person lives by faith in all aspects of his life, including entering into the life of the Spirit.[6]

In each of the passages below, identify the moral failing of Babylon and the judgment awaiting her because of that failing.

Habakkuk 2:6–8

Moral failing

Impending judgment

Habakkuk 2:9–11

Moral failing

Impending judgment

FAITH ALIVE

Keys to Wise Living (Hab. 2:9). The worldly theory of success that centers on personal power and the amassing of financial riches is a highly deceptive trap. The wise person defines success in the light of God's plan for his life. Living in a manner that honors God and relies on His promises brings success.

Know that success by the world's measure is a vain pursuit. Build your house—your life and vocation—on the rock of God's Word. Plan your life by the wisdom of God. Be a success in Him.[7]

Habakkuk 2:12–14

    Moral failing

    Impending judgment

Habakkuk 2:15–17

    Moral failing

    Impending judgment

Habakkuk 2:18, 19

    Moral failing

 FAITH ALIVE

    A Step to Holiness (Hab. 2:18–20). Though some only think of idols as material images, what truly defines an idol is the place it occupies in a person's life. Any person, thing, or desire that stands in the way of an immediate, wholehearted "Yes, Lord!" to anything He asks of us is an idol and must be eliminated.

    Examine yourself! Ask the question, "Is there anything in my life that hinders my obedience to God?" Take down any idol in your life by humbling yourself before God and by refusing other interests to rule your heart.[8]

What would eventually be the reaction of all the nations to mighty, "invincible" Babylon? (Hab. 2:6a)

What eventually would be the reaction of all the nations, including Babylon, to the Lord? (Hab. 2:20)

FAITH ALIVE

How does moral corruption around us challenge our resolve to trust God?

In your opinion, what "idols" in modern society draw people away into immorality?

What can Christians do to keep their faith strong and active in a society that tolerates and flaunts immorality?

TRUST IN THE GOD OF HISTORY

Comparing the beginning and end of the Book of Habakkuk reveals tremendous spiritual growth on the part of the prophet. Initially he could only see the faithlessness of God's people. Finally he only cared to see the faithfulness of the Lord to His people through the whole panorama of the history of salvation.

The prayer of Habakkuk in the third chapter of his prophecies begins and ends with comments which link this poem in structure with the Psalms. In Habakkuk 3:2 what did the prophet admit, and what two things did he ask the Lord to do?

Habakkuk's admission

Habakkuk's two requests

The majority of Habakkuk's prayer affirms the activity of the Lord in the history of His people. Habakkuk 3:3–8 describes the appearance of the Lord to be with His people. Compare Habakkuk 3:3 with Deuteronomy 33:2 (Teman was the capital of Seir, that is, Edom) and identify the likely historical appearance of the Lord that Habakkuk had in mind.

According to the following topics, describe the coming of the Lord to His people. (Hab. 3:3–7)

His glory (vv. 3, 4)

His control of disease (v. 5)

His impact on nature (v. 6)

His impact on opponents of His people (vv. 6b, 7)

The part of Habakkuk's prayer recorded in 3:8–15 describes the action of the Lord as a warrior on behalf of His people through their history. Is the Lord waging war against nature when He causes natural calamities? Why or why not? (Hab. 3:8, 9a)

What effect does the Lord's warfare have on the physical creation? (Hab. 3:9b–11)

What is the real purpose of the Lord's intervention in historical events? (Hab. 3:12–15)

With regard to His people (v. 13)

With regard to His opponents (vv. 12, 14, 15)

 WORD WEALTH

Your Anointed (Hab. 3:13). The terms used here join the idea of salvation with the Lord's Anointed. The Hebrew roots of these words reflect the two names of our Lord: Jesus, meaning "Salvation," and Christ, meaning "the Anointed One."

The context here is God's great power manifested in behalf of His people through a Davidic King to bring them deliverance from their enemies. The Messiah came in the fullness of time (2:3; Gal. 4:4), was given the name "Jesus" as a prenatal prophecy of His ministry (Matt. 1:21), and was born "in the city of David a Savior, which is Christ the Lord" (Luke 2:11).[9]

How did Habakkuk summarize his initial reaction to the idea that the Lord was coming in his day as a warrior to exercise judgment on Judah through the Babylonians? (Hab. 3:16)

According to the following topics, describe the conclusion Habakkuk was able to reach about the impending judgment of God on his people. (Hab. 3:17–19)

The anticipated hardships (v. 17)

The promised attitude (v. 18)

The confident expectation (v. 19)

WORD WEALTH

Joy (Hab. 3:18) translates a Hebrew word that contains the suggestion of "dancing for joy" or "leaping for joy." The verb originally meant "to spin around with intense motion." This lays to rest the notion that the biblical concept of joy is only "a quiet, inner sense of well-being."

God dances for joy over Jerusalem and because of His people (Is. 65:19; Zeph. 3:17). The righteous Messiah shall rejoice in God's salvation with an intensity that the psalmist cannot find words to describe (Ps. 21:1). In turn, His redeemed citizens are joyful in their King; they praise Him with dances, with instruments, and with singing (Ps. 149:2, 3). Although everything is wrong in Habakkuk's external world, he is leaping for joy over his fellowship with Yahweh.[10]

FAITH ALIVE

The Life of Faith (Hab. 2:4; 3:16–19). When all the circumstances of our life present a negative picture—in failure and loss or when the natural reaction would be grief or complaint—this is the time to put faith in God and in His Word. Thus we can see through God's eyes to the final glorious outcome. This brings worship and praise even before our circumstances have changed.

Determine to praise and worship and thank God for His faithfulness, no matter how devastating the circumstances. Look with the eye of faith at God's plan for the future.[11]

Through what difficulties has the Lord taught you to trust Him more deeply?

How do you know the Lord more intimately because of the difficulties that have strengthened your faith?

What difficulties can you see coming or do you dread coming that would once again stretch and strain your faith in the Lord?

What have you learned from Habakkuk's approach to impending disasters that can help you cope with the trials of life?

1. Philip Yancey, "Happy Memories of Bad Times," *Christianity Today* (March 8, 1993), 88.

2. Ibid.

3. *Spirit-Filled Life Bible* (Nashville: Thomas Nelson Publishers, 1991), 1339, "Introduction: Personal Application."

4. Ibid., 1345, "Truth-in-Action through Habakkuk."

5. Ibid., 1341, note on Habakkuk 2:4.

6. Ibid., 1339–1340, "Habakkuk: Introduction, Personal Application; The Holy Spirit at Work."

7. Ibid., 1345, "Truth-in-Action through Habakkuk."

8. Ibid.

9. Ibid., 1339, "Habakkuk: Introduction, Christ Revealed."

10. Ibid., 1344, "Word Wealth: Hab. 3:18 joy."

11. Ibid., 1345, "Truth-in-Action through Habakkuk."

Lesson 10/The Truth About the Wrath of God
Zephaniah 1—3

Wrath is an intense word about deep-seated, long-lasting anger that takes over and influences all of a person's thoughts and actions. Nobody wants to be around someone who is wrathful. When you were a kid, you probably surprised yourself at least once by making an adult mad at you when you didn't expect it. Worse still, there was probably at least one adult in the neighborhood known for his temper, whom you avoided because he might blow up like a volcano. Worst of all, if you were unfortunate, your neighborhood had a grouch who stayed mad all the time and tormented any children in sight.

The neighborhood grouch is an example of wrath rising out of a bad disposition. This form of wrath can seem trivial when placed beside the wrath of a person seeking revenge, the wrath of an evil personality, the wrath of a righteous man in the face of persistent injustice, or the righteous wrath of God when His holiness has long been deeply offended.

Almost all of the "Twelve Voices for Truth" express some aspect of the wrath of God against arrogant sinners. Zephaniah highlights God's wrath in the climactic "day of the LORD."

THE SEARCHING LIGHT OF WRATH

When Zephaniah delivered his blistering message, the iniquity of Judah was nearly full. There was only a tiny window of opportunity for repentance to avert the gathering storm clouds of wrath. The Lord was preparing a thorough, angry housecleaning.

Both the prophet Zephaniah and King Josiah were three generations removed from their common ancestor King

Hezekiah (Zeph. 1:1). What would have been the blood relationship of Zephaniah and Josiah?

BEHIND THE SCENES

Zephaniah gives the general time of his writing as being "in the days of Josiah, the son of Amon, king of Judah" (1:1), about 640 to 609 B.C. The height of Josiah's reform was in the 620s. Since the fall of Nineveh in 612 B.C. had not yet taken place (2:13–15), most scholars set the date of writing between 630 and 627 B.C. His contemporaries included Jeremiah and Nahum.[1]

How will the wrath of God affect all of His creation on the day of the Lord? How will mankind's special place in creation affect their experience of God's wrath? (Zeph. 1:2, 3)

How had Jerusalem and Judah especially provoked the wrath of God? (Zeph. 1:4–6)

BEHIND THE SCENES

Using poetic language (Zeph. 1:2–6), Zephaniah prophesies a worldwide judgment, which includes an erring Judah (vv. 4, 6). His prophecy is partially fulfilled in the fall of Jerusalem in 587 B.C. Its broader intent, however, refers to God's dealing with both His spiritual and physical enemies throughout history. This would be especially true during the time of the Messiah, ultimately finding its consummation in the world to come. Because of its poetry and eschatological intent, Zephaniah often speaks with fluid language whose meaning should not be pressed with strict literalness. Also, precise historical fulfillment of prophesied events is not always easy to determine.[2]

When God first announced the day of the Lord through Zephaniah, how did He describe it? (Zeph. 1:7)

    WORD WEALTH

Day occurs more than 2,200 times in the Old Testament with a variety of meanings in their contexts. "Day" occurs first in Genesis 1:5, where God called the light "Day"; the remainder of the verse shows that day is not only the period of light, but also a period consisting of evening and morning. (Because God placed evening before morning throughout the week of Creation, the Jewish day begins at sundown.)

"Day" may represent a time period or the occasion of a major event. "Day of trouble" (Zeph. 1:15) is thus a troubled time. In Genesis 3:5 and Isaiah 12:4, "day" expresses an indefinite future time. *Yom Yahweh* ("day of the LORD") refers to a time when God reveals Himself through judgment and supernatural events. "The day of the LORD" may also refer to the return of the Lord Jesus to judge and rule the world.[3]

According to the following topics, describe what will occur in Jerusalem on the day of the Lord. (Zeph. 1:7–13)

Those deserving punishment (vv. 8, 9)

The mourning (vv. 10, 11)

    BEHIND THE SCENES

The Fish Gate (Zeph. 1:10) was in the northeast wall of the city, so called because fish from Jordan and Galilee passed through it. The Second Quarter was the upper city, populated by the upper class, overlooking the temple near the main commercial center.[4]

Those bearing special guilt (vv. 12, 13)

 FAITH ALIVE

Steps to Dynamic Devotion (Zeph. 1:12; 3:5). The key to knowing God is to continually seek Him. The chief danger in this quest is the temptation to be satisfied with past encounters so that no fresh pursuits are made. Complacency is the enemy of spiritual growth.

Remain zealous. Refuse complacency. Seek God faithfully every day. Trust that the Lord behaves justly. Keep your appointments with the Father.[5]

According to the following topics, describe the nature of the day of the Lord. (Zeph. 1:14–20)

Its timing (v. 14)

Its characteristics (vv. 15, 16)

Its effects (vv. 17, 18; see vv. 2, 3)

According to the following topics, describe the only appropriate response to the prospect of the "searching light" of God's wrath. (Zeph. 2:1–3)

Physical aspect of the response (v. 1)

Spiritual aspects of the response (v. 3a)

Possible results of the response (v. 3b)

FAITH ALIVE

What do you think makes spiritual complacency so deadly to true spiritual vitality?

How can spiritual complacency lead to the need for divine chastening?

What are some ways you can guard against such complacency?

List spiritual and practical ways you can combat the following violations of God's law in your community. (See 1 Chr. 7:14; Dan. 9:3–6; Eph. 6:10–18)

Injustice

Violence

Immorality

Idolatry

THE VENGEFUL ROD OF WRATH

Centuries after Zephaniah, Peter wrote, "For the time has come for judgment to begin at the house of God; and if it begins with us first, what will be the end of those who do not obey the gospel of God?" (1 Pet. 4:17). On the day of the Lord, the wrath of God will be a searching light among His people; but among the unbelieving nations the wrath of God will be a rod of vengeance.

How will the wrath of day of the Lord affect the Philistine cities to the west of Judah? (Zeph. 2:4–7)

On the short term (vv. 4, 5)

On the long term (vv. 6, 7)

 BEHIND THE SCENES

The remnant (Zeph. 2:7) refers in part to the returnees from the Babylonian captivity. In a broader sense, it refers to God's yet future church. To some biblical scholars, this also refers to a Jewish remnant who will physically occupy an end-times national Israel.[6]

How will the wrath of day of the Lord affect the nations of Moab and Ammon to the east of Judah? (Zeph. 2:8–11)

In the short term (vv. 8, 9)

In the long term (vv. 10, 11)

 BEHIND THE SCENES

Moabites and Ammonites (Zeph 2:8–11), both descendants of Lot, were neighboring nations located near the sites of Sodom and Gomorrah on the east side of the Dead Sea. Reproach, insults, and arrogant threats against the people of the Lord of hosts were made by these two bitter enemies. They had shown their arrogance periodically by violating Israel's borders; now the weakness of Judah has given them occasion for contempt.[7]

How will the wrath of day of the Lord affect the Ethiopians to the south of Judah? (Zeph. 2:12)

How will the wrath of day of the Lord affect the Assyrians to the north of Judah? (Zeph. 2:13–15)

In the long term (vv. 13, 14)

In the short term (v. 15)

BEHIND THE SCENES

Geographically Assyria was more east than north of Judah, but Assyrian armies always came from due north. Consequently Assyria was always thought of as a northern power. Nothing seemed more improbable than that Assyria, which had literally carried off ten northern tribes, would itself become a desolation. Walls 100 feet high encompassed Nineveh for sixty miles. The walls were so wide that three chariots abreast could ride on them. With its 1,500 watchtowers, Nineveh felt justified to boast, "there is none besides me" (v. 15).[8]

FAITH ALIVE

Does the Lord seem more upset with His people (Zeph. 1) or with the unbelieving nations (Zeph. 2)? What lessons can you draw from this?

As shown in Zephaniah 2, what are the kinds of things that disturb the Lord in the conduct of nations?

THE PURIFYING FLAME OF WRATH

The wrath of God is never a blind rage that lashes out vindictively and pettily in mindless fury. The wrath of God punishes and purifies: punishes the enemies of God and purifies His rebellious children. The nation of Israel will suffer terribly on the day of the Lord, but out of that day emerges a holy remnant who will serve Him faithfully forever.

Describe the rebellion and pollution of Jerusalem that will provoke the wrath of the day of the Lord. (Zeph. 3:1, 2)

According to the following topics, describe the iniquity of the leaders of Jerusalem before the day of the Lord. (Zeph. 3:3–7)

Civil leaders (v. 3)

Spiritual leaders (v. 4)

Rejection of the Lord (v. 5)

Indifference to warnings (vv. 6, 7)

 FAITH ALIVE

Lessons for Leaders (Zeph. 3:2–4). The wise leader accepts the Scripture's testimony and rejects the prevailing humanistic doctrine that teaches man's intrinsic goodness. An unteachable attitude is the tip of the iceberg of ungodliness. This wisdom should influence one's self-view, causing all of us to guard ourselves from insincerity and pride in any of its manifestations.

Leaders, understand that the clearest evidence that someone does not trust the Lord or seek Him diligently is a rebellious, disobedient, and unteachable nature.

Leaders, avoid being among those who speak loudly, who promise great things, but produce nothing that lasts or bears fruit in the long run.

Leaders, avoid diligently any form of arrogance or pride in your ministry. Do not profane the ministry by mishandling God's Word in any way. Never teach your own opinion as God's Word.[9]

Why did the Lord urge the faithful remnant to wait for the day of the Lord? (Zeph. 3:8; see 1:2, 3 and Hab. 2:3)

In each of the following verses of Zephaniah 3, what benefit awaits the faithful remnant of the people of God following the purifying flame of God's wrath?

v. 9

v. 10

v. 11

v. 12

v. 13

 PROBING THE DEPTHS

The Holy Spirit at Work (Zeph. 3:9). A joyous work of the Holy Spirit is found in the promise that God will restore to the peoples a pure language that they may serve Him with one accord. The curse of Babel was the confusion of languages, which prevented people from working in unity to achieve their evil goals (Gen. 11:1–9). The outpouring of the Spirit promised in Joel 2:28–32 came to pass on the Day of Pentecost (Acts 2:1–11) to begin God's process of messianic restoration. In light of Zephaniah's prophecy, it is interesting to note that Pentecost included the dimension of languages.

Furthermore, the gift of tongues was used to bring believing Gentiles and astonished Jews together in unity of faith and purpose during Peter's reluctant visit to the home of Cornelius (Acts 10:44–48). It is this pure language, this gift of tongues, that has also served to merge believers of widely divergent theological persuasions into the modern charismatic movement. They have been enabled to transcend boundaries of tradition and nationality and serve the Lord together in unity of the Spirit. These may be partial fulfillments of Zephaniah 3:9.[10]

        FAITH ALIVE

Growth in Godliness (Zeph. 3:9–13). The sin of pride is most often revealed by the words that we speak. Language becomes unclean with repeated expressions of self-will or the profane use of God's name. Purify your heart, and your speech will be pure also. Allow God to purify your lips and your language.[11]

These verses invite us to review our lives and the purifying work God desires to continue within us. For the following virtues, answer these questions: How is God prompting you to growth? What personal disciplines could you adopt to cooperate with God's prompting to grow?

A pure language (v. 9)

Offerings (v. 10)

Humility (v. 11)

Trust (v. 12)

Righteousness (v. 13)

Truth (v. 13)

According to each of the following verses in Zephaniah 3, what will the purified remnant of God's people have to sing for joy about when the day of the Lord ushers in the messianic age?

v. 15

v. 16

v. 17

BEHIND THE SCENES

Zephaniah describes God's victory and admiration of His redeemed people (Zeph. 3:17). As Victor, He will be a Hero who helps ("The Mighty One will save"). His love will be seen as deeply felt thoughtfulness and admiration ("He will quiet *you* with His love"). His satisfaction with His people will be expressed through loud, demonstrative singing ("He will rejoice over you with singing").[12]

In each of these concluding verses of Zephaniah 3, what promises does God make to His people who will undergo the purifying flame of His wrath during the day of the Lord?

v. 18

v. 19

v. 20

FAITH ALIVE

Hebrews 11:31 states that "it is a fearful thing to fall into the hands of the living God." How does Zephaniah's description of the wrath of the day of the Lord verify the truth of the statement in Hebrews?

How do you understand the wrath of God as described in the Bible to differ from human wrath as you have seen it expressed by people around you?

What does God want to accomplish when He pours out this wrath?

How do you react to the idea that God might sing today over you because He loves and saves you? (Zeph. 3:17)

1. *Spirit-Filled Life Bible* (Nashville: Thomas Nelson Publishers, 1991), 1346, "Introduction: Date."

2. Ibid., 1350, note on Zephaniah 1:2–6.

3. Ibid., "Word Wealth: Zeph. 1:7 day."

4. Ibid., 1351, note on Zephaniah. 1:10.

5. Ibid., 1355, "Truth-in-Action through Zephaniah."

6. Ibid., 1352, note on Zephaniah 2:7.

7. Ibid., note on Zephaniah 2:8–11.

8. Ibid., 1353, note on Zephaniah 2:13–15.

9. Ibid., 1355, "Truth-in-Action through Zephaniah."

10. Ibid., 1349, "Zephaniah: Introduction, The Holy Spirit at Work."

11. Ibid., 1355, "Truth-in-Action through Zephaniah."

12. Ibid., 1354, note on Zephaniah 3:17.

Lesson 11/The Truth About Courage
Haggai 1, 2 and Zechariah 1—8

During the dark days of Fascist expansion in Europe and the bloody days of the Second World War, writer J.R.R. Tolkien created an alternative world he called Middle Earth. Populated by elves, dwarves, and hobbits, as well as men, Middle Earth also faced dark forces that threatened to plunge the land into totalitarian darkness. Against the threat posed by evil, Tolkien imagined a resistance composed largely of the heroism of men and the dogged courage of hobbits.

Interestingly, when we read *The Hobbit* or *The Lord of the Rings,* we may identify with the hobbits rather than with the humans. The men are characters of mythic proportion, but the hobbits are creatures who love hearth and home, a good meal and a soft bed, sunshine and autumn leaves, friends and family, and an ordered community life without outside interference.

Hobbits are small creatures, too harmless to pay much attention to, but when the dark powers of Middle Earth begin to disturb the hobbits of the Shire, these gentle folk prove unexpectedly courageous. At story's end, while massive armies clash before great walled cities, and plots and plans swirl around the land, a lone hobbit drags himself into the desolate fortress of Evil and unmakes It with an act of courageous self-sacrifice absolutely unexpected and incomprehensible to the mind behind the wickedness.

Courage always has a touch of facing the bully. In the name of the Lord, the prophets Haggai and Zechariah told the remnant of Judah who had returned from the Babylonian captivity that it was time for courage. It was time to stop hiding behind their smallness and inadequacy and act on the promises and commands of the Lord.

THE COURAGE OF SMALL BEGINNINGS

In four months of the year 520 B.C. the prophet Haggai conducted his brief but focused ministry. Fifteen years earlier the first organized party of Jewish exiles had returned from the seventy-year Babylonian exile and begun enthusiastically to rebuild God's covenant community. But the original motivation had quickly waned, and pursuit of the plans of God had been replaced by petty self-interests. Hope in God had given way to cynicism.

 AT A GLANCE

Complete the following time chart for the prophecies and events recorded in the Book of Haggai.

REFERENCE	BIBLICAL CALENDAR	MODERN CALENDAR
Hag. 1:1	_____	Aug. 29, 520 B.C.
Hag. 1:15	_____	Sept. 21, 520 B.C.
Hag. 2:1	_____	Oct. 17, 520 B.C.
Hag. 2:10	_____	Dec. 18, 520 B.C.
Hag. 2:20	_____	Dec. 18, 520 B.C.[1]

Read quickly through the Book of Haggai and underline or highlight every occurrence of the expression "the word of the LORD came" and circle every occurrence of the phrases "thus says the LORD of hosts" and "says the LORD." Count the number of appearances of these indications of Haggai's self-awareness of God speaking through him and record them below.

"The word of the LORD"   ( )

"Thus says the LORD of hosts"   ( )

"says the LORD"   ( )

TOTAL   ( )

BIBLE EXTRA

Read the account in Ezra 3 and 4 of the beginning of spiritual organization by the returned exiles at Jerusalem in 536 B.C. Summarize your findings about each of these topics.

Renewed worship (3:1–7)

Temple construction (3:8–13)

Halt to temple construction (4:1–24)

Why do you think the Lord directed His first prophecy through Haggai to Zerubbabel and Joshua? (Hag. 1:1; see Ezra 3, 4)

According to the following topics, analyze the prophetic challenge to rebuild the temple, which was given to the returned exiles of Judah. (Hag. 1:2–11)

The remnant's excuse (v. 2)

The remnant's inconsistency (vv. 3, 4)

The remnant's consequences (vv. 5, 6, 9–11)

The remnant's solution (vv. 7, 8)

How did each of the following respond to the challenge of the Lord to rebuild His temple in Jerusalem? (Hag. 1:12–15)

Zerubbabel and Joshua (vv. 12, 14)

Haggai (v. 13)

The populace (v. 14)

According to the following topics, describe the second prophetic message of Haggai to the remnant of the exiles after a month of preparing the initial stages of temple rebuilding. (Hag. 2:1–9)

The psychological obstacle to rebuilding (v. 3, see Ez. 3:12, 13)

The spiritual solution (vv. 4, 5)

The promise (v. 6–9)

 FAITH ALIVE

Haggai 2:5 explains how the Spirit of God is meant to interact with the spirit of the people in order to get His work accomplished. Verse 5 includes these significant points:

1. The Holy Spirit is a vital part of God's covenant with His people, *"according to* the word that I covenanted with you."

2. The Holy Spirit is an abiding gift to the people of God: "My Spirit remains among you."

3. The presence of the Holy Spirit removes fear from the hearts of God's people. Therefore, "Do not fear!"

These principles remain the same for the people of God today. At the heart of God's covenant with His people is the constant operation of the Holy Spirit, working to release them from fear, so that they may move boldly in fulfilling the divine commission.[2]

According to Haggai 2:10–14, what would be the spiritual condition of each of the following?

Holy food that touched common food

Holy food touched by an unclean person

The remnant after contact with Babylon

The temple built by the remnant

Offerings made in the rebuilt temple

How had the affairs of life for the remnant demonstrated their uncleanness? (Hag. 2:15–17)

How would events following December 18, 520 B.C. demonstrate that the Lord had freely and graciously cleansed the remnant of the exiles from all uncleanness? (Hag. 2:18, 19)

What did Haggai prophecy about Prince Zerubbabel, a descendant of David, that looked forward to the Messiah? (Hag. 2:20–23)

 FAITH ALIVE

The challenge to faith is the same in every generation: seek first the things of God and trust Him to provide the daily necessities of life. The glorification of any work we pursue comes by the presence of God in it. God calls us to commit what we are, what we have, and all that we do to Him.

Make the work of God a priority, both with your time and with your money. Understand that it is the presence of Jesus that produces glory. See 2 Cor. 3:18.

> Choose to believe and reckon as true that when we turn from selfish ambition and personal agenda to focus on advancing God's kingdom, He will bless us toward that end.[3]

Compare the prophecies of Haggai with the words of Jesus in Matthew 6:25–34. What stands out to you for living today?

How do you think the Spirit of God shows His people when it is time to wait patiently on the Lord and when it is time to step forward in faith and dare the impossible?

What current challenges to faith do you face?

Is the Lord directing you to wait or to move forward in faith?

THE COURAGE OF WAITING ON THE LORD

In between the first and second prophecies of Haggai, the Lord also began to speak through Zechariah to the remnant of the exiles who had returned to Jerusalem with Zerubbabel the prince and Joshua the priest. While Haggai's main message was "Get with it!" Zechariah's word was, "Keep expecting more from the Lord."

 ## AT A GLANCE

Complete the following time chart for the prophecies recorded in the first half of the Book of Zechariah.

REFERENCE	BIBLICAL CALENDAR	MODERN CALENDAR
Zech. 1:1	_____	Oct., 520 B.C.
Zech. 1:7	_____	Feb. 15, 519 B.C.
Zech. 7:1	_____	Dec. 7, 518 B.C.

What did the Lord want the remnant of the exiles to learn from the experience of their ancestors on whom the captivity had fallen? (Zech. 1:2–6a; see Jer. 35:15)

What was the response of Zechariah's listeners to his first recorded prophecy? (Zech 1:6b)

 FAITH ALIVE

Anything that God has said He will do, He will do. He does not make empty promises or vain threats. We must not interpret His patience and longsuffering toward disobedience as a failure to execute judgment. Rather, He desires our repentance and return. If we will return to Him, He will complete the work of perfecting what He has promised.[4]

On February 15, 519 B.C. (Zech. 1:7), Zechariah had a series of eight night visions. How did the Lord reveal to the prophet the meanings of these visions? (vv. 9, 14, 19, etc.)

ZECHARIAH'S VISIONS (1:7)[5]	
The Visons of Zechariah had historical meaning for his day, but they also have meaning for all time. God will save His people and bring judgment on the wicked.	
Vision	**Significance**
Man and horses among the myrtle trees (1:8)	The Lord will again be merciful to Jerusalem (1:4, 16, 17)
Four horns, four craftsmen (1:18–20)	Those who scattered Judah are cast out (1:21).
Man with measuring line (2:1)	God will be a protective wall of fire around Jerusalem (2:3–5).
Cleansing of Joshua (3:4)	The Servant, the Branch, comes to save (3:8, 9).
Golden lampstand and olive trees (4:2, 3)	The Lord empowers Israel by His Spirit (4:6)
Flying scroll (5:1)	Dishonesty is cursed (5:3)
Woman in the basket (5:6, 7)	Wickedness will be removed (5:9)
Four chariots (6:1)	The spirits of heaven execute judgment on the whole Earth (6:5, 7)

The visions appear to be arranged so that the first and last develop the same theme, as do the second and sixth, the third and seventh, and the fourth and fifth. The fourth and fifth visions form the heart of the series in importance as well as in layout. Observe how the ideas of the eight visions move from background concepts right into the heart of the matter for Zechariah's audience.

Summarize the first and eighth of Zechariah's night visions and point out the common theme.

Vision 1 (Zech. 1:7–17)

Vision 8 (Zech. 6:1–8)

Common theme

 BEHIND THE SCENES

The Angel of the Lord (Zech. 1:11, 12; 3:1, 5, 6) probably was a preincarnate appearance of the Second Person of the Trinity. In Zechariah 3:2 the Angel of the Lord is referred to as "the LORD," who in turn speaks of "the LORD" as a separate Person. The Angel of the Lord appears in several places in the Old Testament with this same God-in-visible-form motif (see Gen. 16:7–13; 22:11, 12; Judg. 6:11, 22; 13:21–23).

Summarize the second and sixth of Zechariah's night visions and point out the common theme.

Vision 2 (Zech. 1:18–21)

Vision 6 (Zech. 5:1–4)

Common theme

Summarize the third and seventh of Zechariah's night visions and point out the common theme.

Vision 3 (Zech. 2:1–13)

Vision 7 (Zech. 5:5–11)

Common theme

Summarize the fourth and fifth of Zechariah's night visions and point out the common theme.

Vision 4 (Zech. 3:1–10)

Vision 5 (Zech. 4:1–14)

Common theme

  FAITH ALIVE

As governor of Judah, Zerubbabel was ultimately responsible for rebuilding the temple, but he was forbidden to trust the resources of man to accomplish the task. So today God's holy temple, the church, must be built and sustained, not by wealth, by members, by virtue, nor by sheer strength, but "by My Spirit."[6]

Why do you think the visions about Joshua and Zerubbabel would mean the most to Zechariah's listeners?

FAITH ALIVE

Zechariah 4:6, 7 is one of the most often quoted passages in the Old Testament. Copy the verses:

What message do these verses carry for you in your
present circumstance?

BEHIND THE SCENES

When the temple is competed, all will acknowledge its
beauty and realize it is not the result of human achievements,
but rather, of God's grace and more grace. "O great mountain"
could be the opposition of the adversaries of the temple project, the discouraged group of builders, or some type of turmoil
among the people. At any rate, God will see to it that it "shall
become a plain." The New Testament use of "mountain" and
Zechariah's obvious allusion to Isaiah 40:4 make this a future
promise as well. The Messiah's future New Testament reign
will see the removal of many "mountains" by God's grace.[7]

FAITH ALIVE

We must learn how to interpret circumstances from
God's standpoint. Do not allow yourself to be discouraged by
"small things." Understand that God does not give the importance we do to the size of things. Be assured that what God
has begun, He will complete in triumph.[8]

According to the following topics, describe the prophetic
ceremony Zechariah was to perform with the gift from the
group of exiles newly returned from Babylon. (Zech. 6:9–15)

The crown (vv. 10, 11, 14)

The prediction (vv. 12, 13; see 3:8)

The conclusion (v. 15)

 FAITH ALIVE

A Lesson in Faith (Zech. 6:10-15). The work of establishing and completing the ultimate temple (His body) is assigned to Jesus, but He wants our participation through obedience to His voice. Our gift becomes a memorial, but the glory is all His.

Understand that Jesus Christ has committed Himself to building His church and to completing it as a manifestation of His glory. Remember that your gift (v. 10) is important to the task and that your privilege is to render all glory to Him (v. 11).[9]

 FAITH ALIVE

When a church waits for God to bless it and make it what He wants, what do you think that church should be expecting God to do with it and for it?

When you wait for the Lord to fulfill His wonderful and glorious promises for His children, what do you think you should be able to expect to receive from Him right away and what should you be willing to wait a long time for?

THE COURAGE FOR JUSTICE AND WITNESS

If the tiny remnant of returned exiles, struggling to rebuild Jerusalem and reintroduce the worship of the Lord in Judah, was ever going to fulfill the grand goals the Lord had predicted for it, they would need great courage. They would need courage to act justly, unlike their ancestors, and they would need courage to be a bold witness to the surrounding nations.

Nearly two years after Zechariah's night visions (Zech. 1:7; 7:1), a delegation from the Jewish community remaining in Babylon came to Jerusalem with a question about their religious calendar. What was it? (Zech. 7:1–3)

What do you think the Lord wanted the Jews to think about on the basis of the questions He asked about their fasting in each of the following verses?

7:5

7:6

7:7

What did the Lord actually want the fasts of His people to be like? (Zech. 8:18, 19)

FAITH ALIVE

Guidelines for Growing in Godliness (Zech. 7:4–7). Godliness involves godly practices from a godly heart. God rebukes those who fast or practice other religious acts to serve their own ends. The godly person keeps an open ear for God's Word, even when it is not pleasant or calls for change.

Make sure that when you fast your motives are unselfish. Accompany your fastings with attitudes and actions of righteousness and obedience.[10]

Along with fasting, however, were matters of justice. What were the components of justice that the Lord commanded through Zechariah? (Zech. 7:9, 10)

What had happened when Judah had ignored the call of the law and the Spirit to live justly? (Zech. 7:11–14)

The Lord was zealous for restored Jerusalem (Zech. 8:2). According to each of the following topics, how did He express His zeal for the still-struggling community? (Zech. 8:3–8)

Names (v. 3)

Inhabitants (v. 4, 5)

Perspective (v. 6)

Future (vv. 7, 8)

According to the Lord, how could the struggling remnant community in Jerusalem find spiritual strength by looking to the past, present, and future? (Zech 8:9–13)

From the past (vv. 9, 10)

At the present (v. 11)

Into the future (vv. 12, 13)

What were the things the Lord wanted the restoration community in Jerusalem not to be afraid to do? (Zech. 8:14–17)

What did the Lord say would be the responses if the restored community in Jerusalem would live justly according to the law and the Spirit? (Zech. 8:20–23)

To one another (vv. 20, 21)

To God (v. 22)

To the Jews (v. 23)

 ### FAITH ALIVE

Why is it easier for us to feel religious when we are keeping rules than when we are pursuing justice and a loving witness?

If the Lord were going to write down what He is zealous to see happen in your life, what do you think it would be?

How do you need to exercise courage and live more justly in order to draw those who observe your life to the Lord?

---

1. Dates based on Joyce G. Baldwin, *Haggai, Zechariah, Malachi: An Introduction and Commentary* (Downers Grove: Inter-Varsity Press, 1972), 29.

2. *Spirit-Filled Life Bible* (Nashville: Thomas Nelson Publishers, 1991), 1358, "Zechariah: Introduction, The Holy Spirit at Work."

3. Ibid., 1361, "Truth-in-Action through Haggai."

4. Ibid., 1379, "Truth-in-Action through Zechariah."

5. Ibid., 1365, chart on "Zechariah's Visions."

6. Ibid., 1368, note on Zechariah 4:6.

7. Ibid., note on Zechariah 4:7.

8. Ibid., 1380, "Truth-in-Action through Zechariah."

9. Ibid.

10. Ibid.

Lesson 12/The Truth About Hope
Zechariah 9—14

The apostle Paul wrote to the Corinthian Christians that "knowledge puffs up, but love edifies" (1 Cor. 8:1). The Corinthians, like many of the early churches, prized knowledge as an evidence of superiority. Eventually pseudo-Christian sects, collectively known as Gnostics, formed around secret non-biblical doctrines that only members who had served an apprenticeship were allowed to know. The Gnostics considered themselves better than Christians because of what they knew.

Christians of every age have been vulnerable to the spirit of the Gnostics. There will always be those who take inordinate pride in knowledge. One of the areas of biblical doctrine that lends itself to abuse by those in search of prideful knowledge is eschatology, the study of end-time prophecy.

The Lord did not give revelation about the future to amaze or entertain His people. He gave futuristic prophecy to stimulate hope and perseverance among the faithful in the face of trials and persecution. It is the devil who tempts us to try to see the future in order to gain power and to control people. Then, instead of delivering on his evil promises of power, the devil tries to harm those who seek to know the future for selfish reasons.

Zechariah contains some wonderful prophecies of the future. They were meant to give hope to the returned exiles from Babylon as they struggled with the harsh realities of life in a province of the Persian Empire. His readers were never supposed to get puffed up in their minds but built up in their expectation of the vindication of their confidence in God.

HOPE SUFFERS RESOLUTELY

None of the prophecies in Zechariah 9—14 is dated. Apparently some time passed between the prophecies in the first half of the book, which are tied directly to the situation facing Zerubbabel the prince, Joshua the high priest, and the rest of the people of Judah. The last portion of Zechariah is futuristic and independent of references to living people and current events.

Picture the Messiah entering the Holy Land from the north. According to Zechariah 9:1–10, what will happen to each nation as the King comes to Jerusalem in the future?

The cities of Syria and Lebanon (vv. 1, 2)

The island fortress of Tyre (vv. 3, 4)

The cities of the Philistines (v. 5–8)

Jerusalem (vv. 9, 10)

 ### BEHIND THE SCENES

The Lord of Lords or a Rabbi on a Colt? (Zech. 9:9). This is the prophecy of the Lord's Triumphal Entry. We find accounts of its fulfillment in Matthew 21:1–11; Mark 11:1–11; Luke 19:28–44; and John 12:12–19. In this verse we see again how much God's ways differ from man's. Men looked for a conquering king, high and exalted, to come and deliver Jerusalem with an army of mighty men.

What they saw was a meek and lowly Rabbi, riding upon a donkey's colt, and attended by a crowd of rejoicing peasants. He did not look like a conqueror. Yet one week later He had risen from the dead, having conquered death and hell.[1]

According to the following topics, describe the hope of Israel in the messianic kingdom. (Zech. 9:11—10:1)

For the exiles still in Babylon (9:11, 12)

For the returned exiles in Jerusalem facing the emerging power of Greece (9:13)

In end-time battles (9:14–16)

In end-time prosperity (9:17; 10:1)

How did the existing leaders of Jerusalem contrast with the future messianic King? (Zech. 10:2, 3)

   FAITH ALIVE

    A Lesson for Leaders (Zech. 10:2). Remember that God's Word is always true! Teach God's Word faithfully so that the long-term result will be fruitfulness and well being. Leaders, understand that false prophecies, teaching that is erroneous or diluted, and personal opinion taught as truth all result in a church that lacks power, stability, and security.[2]

According to the following topics, describe how the Lord will strengthen Israel in the future. (Zech 10:4–12)

Through the house of Judah (vv. 4, 5)

By reuniting divided Israel (vv. 6–8)

Through lessons learned in captivity (vv. 9, 10)

By personally leading them home (vv. 11, 12)

Before the hope of the wonderful benefits of the reign of the messianic King could be experienced, He would be rejected and His people would suffer. How does the poem in Zechariah 11:1–3 describe the destruction that would enter the Promised Land from the mountains of Lebanon, pass through the pasturelands of Bashan, and move south along the Jordan valley?

In Zechariah 11:4–14, the prophet Zechariah appears to have acted out with literal sheep the role of the Good Shepherd-King that Jesus fulfilled in the Gospels. According to the following topics, how does the good shepherd story in Zechariah parallel the situation Jesus faced?

The attitude of the leaders toward the people (vv. 4–6)

Jesus' attitudes toward the poor and the powerful (vv. 7, 8)

   BEHIND THE SCENES

The identity of the three dismissed shepherds (Zech. 11:8) is impossible to determine. More than three dozen different trios of historical people or groups have been suggested by reputable commentators. Baldwin observes, "Apocalyptic [writing] uses numbers symbolically. Is the number three used in that way here (cf. Dan. 7:8, 24) to signify completion? If so, the good shepherd would be removing from power all the unworthy leaders who frustrated his work."[3]

The results of Israel's rejection of Jesus (vv. 9–11)

The dismissal of the Good Shepherd (vv. 12, 13; see Matt. 26:14, 15; 27:3–10)

The scattering of Israel (v. 14)

 BIBLE EXTRA

Zechariah is sometimes referred to as the most messianic of all the Old Testament books. Chapters 9—14 are the most quoted section of the Prophets in the passion narratives of the Gospels. In the Revelation Zechariah is quoted more than any prophet except Ezekiel.

Zechariah prophesies that the Messiah will come as the Lord's Servant the Branch (3:8), as the Man the Branch (6:12), as both King and Priest (6:13), and as the True Shepherd (11:4–11). He bears eloquent testimony to Christ's betrayal for thirty pieces of silver (11:12, 13), His crucifixion (12:10), His sufferings (13:7), and His Second Advent (14:4).

Two references to Christ are of profound significance. Jesus' triumphal entry into Jerusalem is described in detail in 9:9, four hundred years before the event (see Matt. 21:5; Mark 11:7–10). One of the most dramatic verses of prophetic scriptures is found in 12:10 when in the majority of manuscripts the first person is used: "Then they will look on Me whom they have pierced." Jesus Christ personally prophesied His eventual reception by the house of David.[4]

God promised to raise up a worthless shepherd in the place of the Good Shepherd. No identifiable person is in view, but his ultimate expression will be in the Antichrist. What did Zechariah have to say about the worthless shepherd? (Zech. 11:15–17)

His character (v. 16)

His fate (v. 17)

FAITH ALIVE

How can biblical prophecy, like that in Zechariah, help provide the hope in the Lord that you would need to face suffering and persecution?

daily trials?

witnessing of Christ as Savior?

HOPE TRIUMPHS RESOUNDINGLY

The second "burden" Zechariah delivered to the returned exiles in Jerusalem and Judah (chapters 12—14) covered the same themes as the first "burden" (chapters 9—11). The emphasis shifts, however, to the ultimate triumph of the King who suffered rejection.

Read through Zechariah 12—14 and underline every occurrence of the phrase "in that day." How many did you find? (____)

These chapters focus on the climactic moment when the Messiah comes in triumph.

Before the Messiah comes in triumph, a turning point occurs in Jerusalem and Judah. According to the following topics, describe this important event as recorded in Zechariah 12:1–9.

The relevant character of the Lord (v. 1)

Jerusalem's circumstances (vv. 2, 3)

The Lord's involvement (v. 4)

The leaders' involvement (vv. 5, 6)

The relationship of Judah, Jerusalem, and the house of David (vv. 7, 8)

The physical salvation of Judah and Jerusalem needs to be accompanied by a corresponding spiritual salvation. According to the following topics, describe this important spiritual occurrence as recorded in Zechariah 12:10—13:1.

The spiritual preparation (12:10a)

The spiritual response (12:10b, 11)

The special responsibility of the royal and priestly families (12:12, 13)

The importance of individual repentance (12:14)

The spiritual result of repentance (13:1)

 FAITH ALIVE

The Holy Spirit at Work (Zech. 12:10). Although the reference to *ruach* (spirit/Spirit) is translated by some as God's disposition rather than as the Holy Spirit, others translate it as the Holy Spirit. As such it is one of the most beautiful titles for the Holy Spirit found in Scripture. God's promise is to pour on the house of David and Jerusalem's population "the Spirit of grace and supplication." This immediately precedes their reception and mourning over the One they had pierced. The preparation of the heart by the Holy Spirit is always antecedent to conversion.[5]

How are confession and repentance to be lived out in the life of the Christian today?

How often should these times of repentance take place?

What will be the result in the life of the believer following times of repentance? (13:1)

After true repentance and cleansing occur among the people of Jerusalem and Judah, certain long-standing evil practices will cease. According to the following topics, describe what will happen to false prophets. (Zech 13:2–6)

Their occult connections (v. 2)

Their isolation (v. 3)

Their concealment (v. 4)

Their denial (vv. 5, 6)

 BEHIND THE SCENES

Some ecstatic pagan prophets practiced self-mutilation as part of their rituals (see 1 Kin. 18:28). Zechariah pictured a scene in which a former false prophet claims the scars on his body came from a fight at a friend's house.

All of the wonderful things predicted in Zechariah 12:1—13:6 presupposes the awful scene involving the Good Shepherd portrayed in 13:7–9. According to the following topics, analyze this short poem.

The Lord's role in it all (vv. 7–9)

The Shepherd's destiny (vv. 7)

The immediate effect on the people (vv. 7, 8)

The long-range effect on the people (v. 9)

Zechariah 14 describes in fuller detail the battle of all the nations against Jerusalem and Judah alluded to briefly in 12:1–9. The story here is both grimmer in terms of the indignities Jerusalem suffers and more glorious in terms of the intervention of the Lord. According to the following topics, describe the battle of the day of the Lord. (Zech. 14:1–15)

The plight of Jerusalem (vv. 1, 2)

The arrival of the Lord to do battle (vv. 3, 4)

The escape of Jerusalem (v. 5)

The physical changes caused by the Lord's arrival (vv. 6–11)

The Lord's assault on the besieging nations (vv. 12–15)

The final portion of Zechariah's prophecies concerns the universal worship of the Lord by Gentiles and Jews after the cataclysms of the day of the Lord. How did Zechariah foresee the survivors among the Gentile nations participating in the covenant of God with His people? (Zech. 14:16–19; see Deut. 28:15, 24, 27)

How did Zechariah picture the future time when there would be no distinction between the sacred and the ordinary—all would be holy? (Zech. 14:20, 21)

In work

In worship

In family life

In separation from corruption

 BEHIND THE SCENES

What role does suffering play in Zechariah to prepare Israel for triumph in the day of the Lord?

What role do you think suffering sometimes plays in the lives of believers to prepare them for the triumph the Lord wants them to experience?

What hope for the future has the Holy Spirit stirred in your heart through your study of the Book of Zechariah?

1. *Spirit-Filled Life Bible* (Nashville: Thomas Nelson Publishers, 1991), 1373, "Kingdom Dynamics: Zech. 9:9 The Lord of Lords or a Rabbi on a Colt?"

2. Ibid., 1389, "Truth-in-Action through Zechariah."

3. Joyce G. Baldwin, *Haggai, Zechariah, Malachi: An Introduction and Commentary* (Downers Grove: Inter-Varsity Press, 1972), 183.

4. *Spirit-Filled Life Bible*, 1363–1364, "Zechariah: Introduction, The Holy Spirit at Work."

5. Ibid., 1364.

Lesson 13/The Truth About Mediocrity
Malachi 1—4

Roman Hruska looks like a name you couldn't easily forget, but the chances are it's unfamiliar to you. Hruska was a United States Senator from Nebraska during the days of Richard Nixon's presidency. During one period Nixon struggled to find a highly-respected nominee for Supreme Court justice. Critics accused Nixon of tapping conservative candidates who were undistinguished jurists. Senator Roman Hruska gained his fifteen minutes of fame by suggesting that even the mediocre needed representation on the Supreme Court.

When the exiles from Babylon returned to Jerusalem and Judah after seventy years of captivity, they experienced a great deal of frustration and defeat. Oh, sure, they responded to the divine cheerleading of Haggai and Zechariah to rebuild the temple—on a small scale. Yes, they had finally raised walls around the holy city under the none-too-gentle prodding of Nehemiah.

But on the whole, the exiles in the days of the prophet Malachi were ready to join the guys around Garrison Keillor's campfire or listen to another Johnny Cash song on the jukebox in the corner. They were beaten down and ready to settle for the path of least resistance. They embraced mediocrity as a goal worth easing toward.

MEDIOCRITY CAN'T RECEIVE LOVE

When God tells people that He loves them and they respond, "Yeah, right!" there is a serious spiritual problem at work. That is exactly how the Book of Malachi begins.

Skim the Book of Malachi and summarize why you think the prophet called his message a burden. (Mal. 1:1)

Go back through the book and underline every question that the Lord personally directs to Malachi's readers. How many are there? (_____)

When Israel asked, "In what way have You loved us?" in response to the Lord's declaration of love, how would you interpret the thoughts and assumptions in Israel's mind that prompted their question? (Mal. 1:2)

What evidence from the past did the Lord offer of His love for Israel? (Mal. 1:2b, 3)

What future evidence of His love for Israel did the Lord promise? (Mal. 1:4)

What did the Lord promise He would one day make Israel admit? (Mal. 1:5)

Why do you think that Israel, mired in self-pity and mediocrity, took little notice of the Lord's declaration of love through the prophet Malachi?

  FAITH ALIVE

If you adopt a mediocre standard for your Christian life, how will it impede your sense of God's love for you?

If you revel in the knowledge of God's love for you, how will that knowledge keep you from being satisfied with mediocrity in your Christian life?

MEDIOCRITY CAN'T COMMIT TO LOVE

Not surprisingly, the exiles who had returned to Judah and Jerusalem and lost a sense of God's love for them were unable to muster much love for Him in return. This showed in the way they kept up a superficial religiosity that insulted God.

What was the general charge of the Lord against His priests who set the spiritual tone for the whole people? (Mal. 1:6)

How did the Lord substantiate His charge against the priests? (Mal. 1:7–9)

What situations would be preferable to the mediocre worship offered by the priests? (Mal. 1:10, 11)

What were the specifics of the way the priests defiled the sacrifices offered to the Lord, and why did this bother Him? (Mal. 1:12–14)

What would be the consequences for the priests of their indifferent attitude toward the worship of the Lord? (Mal. 2:1–4a)

What was the ideal the priests were to commit themselves to? (Mal. 2:4b–6)

How did the Lord summarize His complaint against the mediocre priests? (Mal. 2:7–9)

The priests were not alone in having a puny and sickly commitment to the Lord. What was the first way that the general populace of Judah showed their mediocre commitment to the Lord? (Mal. 2:10–12)

FAITH ALIVE

Steps to Covenant Life (Mal. 2:11–16). The covenant relationship of marriage is highly esteemed by the Spirit of God. He instructs believers to seek a believing partner to insure holiness in the marriage. He also requires just and faithful behavior within the marriage bonds. God hates the hard-hearted attitude that destroys this sacred covenant and produces divorce.

Obey God; marry only in the Lord. Be loving and faithful to your marriage partner. Reject divorce as an answer to marital problems. Honor your covenant with God. Trust Him to recover the hope in a seemingly "hopeless" marriage. Be willing to relearn love, understanding, and forgiveness.[1]

What was the second way the average citizens showed their spiritual indifference? (Mal. 2:13–16)

BEHIND THE SCENES

God Backs Up the Covenant of Marriage (Mal. 2:13, 14, 16). When two people marry, God stands as a witness to the marriage, sealing it with the strongest possible word: *covenant.* "Covenant" speaks of faithfulness and enduring commitment. It stands like a divine sentinel over marriage, for blessing or for judgment.

Divorce is here described as *violence.* To initiate divorce does violence to God's intention for marriage and to the mate to whom one has been joined.

Yet where husband and wife live according to their marriage vows, all the power of a covenant-keeping God stands behind them and their marriage. What a confidence, to know that *God backs up our marriage.* His power and authority stand against every enemy that would violently threaten it from without or within.[2]

What spiritual consequences did the people risk because of their mediocre spirituality? (Mal. 2:12, 13)

 FAITH ALIVE

What do you think would happen in the life of believers if they have mediocre commitments to the Lord?

Why do you think Christians resigned to mediocre lives would have trouble truly loving God or one another?

MEDIOCRITY RISKS JUDGMENT

Mediocre lives on the part of God's people prompt the Lord to exercise "tough love" toward them to rejuvenate their commitment to Him. The returned exiles in Jerusalem and Judah needed to realize that they were hastening the discipline of the Lord through their sloppy spiritual lives.

What had happened to the moral vision of the people of Judah because of their lukewarm commitment to God's covenant? (Mal. 2:16, 17)

What would be the ultimate answer to the careless spiritual lives of the returned exiles in Jerusalem and Judah? (Mal. 3:1)

PROBING THE DEPTHS

Malachi's criticism of abuses and religious indifference is still valid today. God's people always need to confess their inadequate response to divine love. Initial devotion to God and enthusiasm may diminish. Genuine worship frequently turns into mechanical observance of religious practices. Delinquent tithing, divorce of faithful spouses, and intermarriage between God's covenant people and nonbelievers often create havoc in families. Selfish desires, combined with proud and arrogant attitudes, lead to serious problems for which God is blamed. Instead of acknowledging our neglect and changing our lives by the power of the Holy Spirit, we ask the question, "Where is the God of justice?" (2:17). However, true repentance still prepares the way for necessary reforms and Holy Spirit-inspired revivals.[3]

BEHIND THE SCENES

The messenger who prepares the way before the Lord is identified in the Gospels as John the Baptist (Matt. 11:10; Mark 1:2; Luke 7:27; all quote the first part of Mal. 3:1). Malachi in his prophecy blends together aspects of both advents of Christ, so that from 3:2 onward the judgment associated with the Second Advent is in view.

According to the following topics, describe the activity of the Messiah at His Second Advent. (Mal. 3:2–5)

His goal (vv. 2)

His effect on the priests (v. 3)

His effect on the people (v. 4)

His effect on sinners (v. 5)

What advantages had inconsistent and half-hearted Israel gained from the changeless nature of the Lord? (Mal. 3:6, 7)

BEHIND THE SCENES

The temple worship of Israel depended absolutely on the tithes of the populace. Tithes were not primarily monetary donations but portions of grain, olive oil, wine, and other agricultural products. In addition, wood had to be supplied to burn or cook offerings. When the tithes were not brought to the temple, the worship of the Lord had to be suspended. This had already happened in the time since the return from Babylon (see Num. 18:21–24; Neh. 10:32–39; 12:44, 47; 13:10–13, 30, 31).

According to the following topics, describe the theft the returned exiles in Jerusalem and Judah had perpetrated against the Lord. (Mal. 3:8–10)

The nature of the theft (v. 8)

The consequences of the theft (v. 9)

The alternative to theft (v. 10)

How did the promised blessing of the Lord on the ones who supported the worship of the Lord go beyond bountiful harvests? (Mal. 3:11, 12)

Why do you suppose the returned exiles were withholding the tithes of their agricultural products?

What does this say about their understanding of the nature of prosperity and blessing?

 FAITH ALIVE

Your Giving Proves God, Opens the Windows of Heaven to You, and Causes the Devourer to Be Rebuked (Mal. 3:10, 11). In this passage of Scripture, God actually invites people to *try* (prove) Him—to verify His trustworthiness with their giving. He says that by withheld giving we rob Him of the privilege of pouring out great and overflowing blessings. He calls for renewed giving with this promise.

First, there will be "food" or resources for God's work ("in My house"). Second, He says those who give will be placed in position to receive great, overflowing blessings. You can experience the windows of heaven actually opening with blessings you will not be able to "receive" or contain! Third, God says that He will "rebuke the devourer" *for your sakes.* He will cause every blessing that has your name written on it to be directed to you, and Satan himself cannot stop it.

Do not be afraid to *prove* God with your giving; He is God and He will stand the test every time.[4]

Mediocre people don't participate in the supernatural aspects of the spiritual life. Too much risk is involved. They tend to become cynical about whether God actually intervenes in anyone's life since they seldom observe Him in their own. How did spiritual cynicism express itself in the lives of the returned exiles in Jerusalem and Judah? (Mal. 3:13–15)

Not everyone in Jerusalem and Judah was a spiritual cynic, however. How did the Lord respond to those who eagerly and enthusiastically feared Him? (Mal. 3:16–18)

On the day of the Lord, what will be the fates of the wicked and the righteous?

The wicked (Mal. 4:1)

The righteous (Mal. 4:2)

   WORD WEALTH

Healing (Mal. 4:2) means restoration of health, remedy, cure, medicine, tranquility, deliverance, or refreshing. Salvation is God's rescue of the entire person, and healing is His complete repair of that person. This noun stems from a verb which in Psalm 41:4 and 147:3 refers to the healing of a soul that has sinned and the healing of a broken heart. In the present reference, the Messiah is compared to a rising sun, which has visible, radiant beams of sunlight streaming outward in all directions. From each of these beams of glorious light, healing flows.[5]

How will the righteous and wicked interact on the day of the Lord? (Mal. 4:3)

   FAITH ALIVE

Mediocrity resists or avoids the purifying work of the Lord. How have you experienced His cleansing activity in your life recently? How did you respond to Him?

Mediocrity resists or avoids investing in the work of God. How do you invest time, talent, and treasure in the kingdom of God? How is your enthusiasm level for God's work?

Mediocrity doesn't really expect God to do anything remarkable. What are you prayerfully expecting of God that must be a supernatural event?

MEDIOCRITY IS UNACCEPTABLE

In Revelation 3:16 the Lord Jesus threatened to spit out the lukewarm Laodicean church because their spiritual mediocrity nauseated Him. The Book of Malachi (and with it the entire Old Testament) ends with a similar stern warning.

The Lord expected the returned exiles in Jerusalem and Judah to look back and to look forward to be cured of their spiritual mediocrity. What were they to look back to and what do you think they were to find there as a cure? (Mal. 4:4)

What were they to look ahead to, and what do you think they were to find there as a cure? (Mal. 4:5)

What were the two alternatives that "Elijah the Prophet" would offer? (Mal. 4:6)

 BEHIND THE SCENES

In conclusion, the prophet admonishes the people to "remember the law of Moses" (Mal. 4:4). Then follows the promise of the coming of Elijah the prophet, earlier referred to as "My messenger" (3:1).

This prophetic utterance closes the Old Testament with the hope of unity and healing. Malachi, like Obadiah and other predecessors, looks with telescopic vision toward Christ's First Advent and salvation for all who believe in Him. But he also views Christ's Second Advent, with the final judgment of the wicked and ultimate salvation of those who fear His name (v. 6).[6]

FAITH ALIVE

To what can you look back to help keep you from getting complacent and lukewarm in your commitment and relationship to Jesus Christ?

To what can you look ahead to help keep you from getting complacent and lukewarm in your commitment and relationship to Jesus Christ?

Look back through your study of *Twelve Voices for Truth*. What aspects of God's truth as presented by the Holy Spirit through the minor prophets do you want to see change your life for a long time to come?

1. *Spirit-Filled Life Bible* (Nashville: Thomas Nelson Publishers, 1991), 1389, "Truth-in-Action through Malachi."

2. Ibid., 1385, "Kingdom Dynamics: Mal. 2:13, 14, 16 God Backs Up the Covenant of Marriage."

3. Ibid., 1382, "Malachi: Introduction, Personal Application."

4. Ibid., 1387, "Kingdom Dynamics: Mal. 3:10, 11 Your Giving Proves God, Opens the Windows of Heaven to You, and Causes the Devourer to Be Rebuked."

5. Ibid., 1388, "Word Wealth: Mal. 4:2, healing."

6. Ibid., note on Mal. 4:4–6.